Grabtown Girl

*Ava Gardner's
North Carolina Childhood
and Her Enduring
Ties to Home*

Doris Rollins Cannon

Down Home Press, Asheboro, N.C.

ISBN 1-878086-89-8
Library of Congress Control Number 2001 131638
Printed in the United States of America

Book design by Beth Hennington
Cover design by Tim Rickard

Down Home Press
P.O. Box 4126, Asheboro, N.C. 27204

Distributed by John F. Blair Publisher
1406 Plaza Dr., Winston-Salem, N.C. 27103

Acknowledgements

Most of the material in this book came from interviews with Ava's family and friends, including many who have died since sharing their memories.

A special thanks to Mary Edna Grimes Grantham and Al Creech of Smithfield, N.C., for supplying names and dates pertinent to Gardner family history, as well as family photos and memories of Ava.

Thanks to Bill Wilson of Raleigh for help with obscure facts and for providing photos from his personal Ava Gardner collection.

Thanks to Col. Henry Royall of Chapel Hill for the early history of Grabtown; and to the Ava Gardner Museum in Smithfield and Eunice Norton, Billie Stevens, and Deidre Kraft for assistance in looking up specific materials in the museum collection.

Thanks to the Johnston County Room of The Heritage Center in Smithfield for use of files and for assistance by Margaret Lee, Ann Tate, and Joan Jones.

For their work on old photographs, thanks to Wayne Weaver Hitt of Morganton, N.C.; John Gregory and Jimmy Wallace of Smithfield; and to Alberta Cooney Luehrs-Fagan of Wilson County, N.C., for sharing Rock Ridge photos made in 1939 and 1978.

Some information was gleaned from *Ava: My Story,* published by Bantam Books in November, 1990, and Old Raleigh Boys Reminisce, (1999) Russ Reynolds, editor/publisher.

Thanks to the *Smithfield Herald* and to the late C.S. Rollins of Haywood County, N.C., who cranked his old jalopy one Sunday in 1951 and took his daughter and her friends to see *Show Boat.*

Contents

Foreword

Part One: **They Knew Her When**
1. The Gardners of Grabtown 11
2. If Only... 17
3. Room for More 21
4. Moving On Down the Road 25
5. Banner Brogden Years 31
6. A Metamorphosis 41
7. Almost Like Going Home 47
8. Winds of Change 61

Part Two: **And They Knew Her Then**
9. Duhan Does a Double Take 69
10. California, Here They Come! 73
11. Uncle Sam and Other Kin 77
12. Sorrow and Success 81
13. Becoming a Star 91
14. The Sinatra They All Loved 97
15. Leaving America 105
16. Incognito 113
17. Rock Ridge Reunion 119
18. The Trying Eighties 125
19. Coming Home to Stay 129
20. Back to Her Sister's Side 133
21. The Ava Gardner Museum 135
Final Thoughts 141

Ava Gardner Filmography 143

Foreword

A number of books have been written about Ava Gardner, one of the great legends of the golden age of the silver screen.

So why another?

The answer is that previous books, including her 1990 autobiography, largely focused on her years as a celebrated actress, her many romances, and her marriages to three famous men.

The aim of *Grabtown Girl* is to tell who Ava Gardner was at root level—a girl who was strengthened by and remained true to her rural North Carolina heritage. She never forgot those who were part of her life before the fateful summer of 1941, when at age eighteen, she and her sister, Bappie, boarded a train bound for Hollywood.

—Doris Rollins Cannon

Part One

They Knew Her When

The Gardners of Grabtown

Long before the "horseless carriage" became a familiar sight on country roads, a salesman who operated a general store on wheels made regular stops in a sparsely settled Johnston County township called Boon Hill in North Carolina's Piedmont.

The merchant hauled his wide range of merchandise in a covered wagon drawn by four horses. When he reached a spot less than two miles from the Neuse River and eight miles from the little town of Smithfield, he tied his horses to a large oak and got down to business.

He would take cash, if his customers were fortunate enough to have any, or he would trade for something that he could sell at other stops along the way—perhaps a few dozen eggs, a generous slab of ham, a fresh bundle of collards.

Inside the wagon was almost anything that country folks might need or want: kerosene lanterns; ropes and bridles; boots and shoes; spools of thread and yarn; bolts of colorful cloth for housewives to turn into dresses, aprons and shirts; blocks of salt to be licked by cattle; and peppermint candy to be licked by children.

So to say that the big covered wagon was a welcome sight as it lumbered into view was a bit of an understatement. And to say that it made regular stops was somewhat misleading.

The man who operated the rolling store no doubt did his best to meet a regular schedule, but on many occasions circumstances caused his customers to wait for hours at the oak—and sometimes the wagon didn't show up until the next day.

But regardless of whether the wagon was on time, when its wheels finally came to a halt, the customers began grabbing for goods.

So it was that the wagon's stopping place became known as Grabtown.

Grabtown never became a real town, or even a very large rural community. It never appeared on a North Carolina map, and it never had a post office. In its heyday in the early decades of the twentieth century, Grabtown had a cotton gin, a cotton seed storage barn and other outbuildings, a sawmill, a tiny store, a number of tenant dwellings, and a white, frame church called T's Chapel, in honor of T.T. Oliver, who had been one of the largest landowners in the area. (In later years, the church would expand and move to another location near Grabtown, and the spelling would be changed to Tee's Chapel.)

A timber company laid a railroad through the area near the beginning of the twentieth century to haul out logs. The tracks reached all the way to the main line in Pine Level, a small town six miles from Grabtown. A spur came right up to Grabtown, where the little store kept supplies needed by the timber workers.

As the tram cars slowly made their way along the tracks, children would grab on and enjoy the thrill of a free ride. Some adults would grab a ride all the way to Pine Level. So Grabtown further earned its name.

Although the exact date is unknown, it is thought that Jonas Bailey Gardner and his wife, Mary Elizabeth, a young couple from Wilson County, moved to Grabtown with their three small daughters sometime in 1907.

Jonas, also called J.B., was born in Wilson County on October 30, 1878. His parents were James Bailey and Elizabeth Dilda Gardner. His father had served in the Confederate Army. Mary Elizabeth, called Mollie, was born in Wilson County on November 21, 1883, the daughter of King David and Elizabeth Forbes Baker. Mollie was less than two months old when her mother died, leaving her in the care of her older sisters, who were not much more than children themselves. Her father soon remarried and had a number of other offspring.

Mollie was nineteen and Jonas twenty-four when they married at the bride's home in the Wilson County community of Saratoga. Amos Chrisp performed the ceremony on January 21, 1903.

Their link to Grabtown was formed the year they became man and wife, although it would be another four years before they moved there. Later that year, they joined Jonas' brother and sister-in-law, Warren and Minnie Gardner of Greene County, in purchasing 300 acres from James H. Pou in Boon Hill Township. The price was $4,500. They bought the land in the hope of securing a prosperous future for themselves and the children they planned to have, the first of whom was already on the way.

Beatrice Elizabeth was born on November 14, 1903, in Wilson County. A second daughter, Elsie Mae, arrived less than a year later on November 2, 1904, followed by a third, Edna Inez, who would be called by her middle name, born on December 15, 1906.

A year before their move to Grabtown, Jonas and Mollie formed a partnership with Jonas' brother, Ben, and his wife, Zilphia, to buy two more large tracts in Boon Hill Township, one 949 acres, the other 438. The tracts, originally known as the Whitley lands, were sold by heirs of T.T. Oliver. The Gardners paid $1,000 down and agreed to pay $1,000 per year for fourteen years, with interest.

Ben's family included seven sons and two daughters, some almost grown by the time they moved to Johnston County. The family lived in a large white-columned house, which retired Army colonel Henry Royall of Chapel Hill, who was born in a Grabtown tenant house in 1904, said was built about 1847 by an ancestor of noted North Carolina historian William Powell and "was as fine as any antebellum house along the Mississippi."

Ben kept a small store on his property, and also had a large stable of mules and horses, a great attraction for youngsters in the area.

One day, young Henry Royall was offered a ride on a horse by classmate Rex Gardner, one of Ben's younger sons. Henry had never ridden a horse. He asked for one that wouldn't buck.

"Rex and two of his brothers went riding too," Henry said. "I was doing fine and my horse was galloping right along with the others, until we came to a wire fence. Then my horse ran right into the fence and my leg went between the fence and a wooden post."

When Henry was thrown off, he landed on his feet, but his leg was gashed nearly to the bone. And he had the dreaded task of explaining to his mother how he got such a wound—and that ugly tear in his long black stocking.

After the accident, Henry learned that he had indeed been

given the gentlest horse in Ben Gardner's stable. The problem was that it was blind.

It is believed that Ben and his family lived in the their antebellum home prior to the arrival of Jonas and Mollie, and that Jonas periodically came from Wilson County and stayed with them while he cut his own lumber at the sawmill to build a two-story frame house with a big front porch for his family.

Not long after Jonas moved his family into their new home, portions of the county seat, Smithfield, were aglow with electric lights, and many townfolks had indoor plumbing. But it would be decades before electric lines reached Grabtown, where water was pulled from wells with a bucket on a rope, or vigorously coaxed out with a hand pump, and toilets were outhouses with pits. Cooking was done on wood or coal stoves.

The older Gardner children, Beatrice and Elsie Mae, attended a one-room school called the Old Hill School, where Henry Royall was one of their classmates. Boys sat on one side of the room and girls on the other, Henry recalled. One day when he misbehaved the teacher came up with an unusual punishment. "She made me sit next to Beatrice," he recalled, "and I liked Beatrice a lot."

The teacher moved him back when she realized how much Henry was enjoying himself. After that, she made him stand in the corner on one foot for punishment.

Henry and Beatrice became fierce competitors in spelling bees and achieving top marks. After they had finished the equivalent of the second grade, the Old Hill School, along with several other one-room schools in the area, was closed, and students moved to a new and larger school at Brogden, about a mile from Grabtown. Old Hill School was converted into a residence and eventually became the home of Henry's parents.

Brogden School, built around 1910, was a wooden structure that served grades one through eight and employed several teachers. It became the focal point of the community. Students often put on shows at the school. A temporary stage would be constructed and bed sheets were used for curtains. Costumes were made by mothers and teachers.

Nearly eighty-four years later, Colonel Royall would fondly

recall one of those shows in which he and Beatrice performed to-gether. He thought they must have been about twelve. They walked slowly across the stage, Henry carrying an open umbrella, Beatrice holding onto his arm as they sang "Under the Old Umbrella." He still remembered all the words:

(Beatrice's solo)
Oh see how black the clouds begin to gather.
Hear the thunder roll and rattle overhead.
Let us hurry up a little—I had rather—
Though I want to say I'm not the least afraid

(Henry's solo)
Gracious me, I thought I felt you tremble,
And your heart it seems to be a trifle weak.
Do not fear, sweet sister mine,
We will reach the school at nine,
If the old umbrella doesn't spring a leak.

(Duet in harmony)
Under the old umbrella,
Safe from the peppering rain.
Under the old umbrella,
Down through the orchard lane,
Crossing the glittering pool—
Under the old umbrella,
Going and coming from school.

If Only...

Jonas Gardner raised cotton and tobacco to make a living for his family and to pay off the debt on the land he and his brothers had bought. Like many farmers, he kept dynamite for clearing tree stumps and other such purposes. Before dawn one February day in 1911, another farmer knocked at the Gardners' door and asked to borrow a few dynamite caps.

Jonas brought out his box of caps, gave the man the number he requested, then placed the box back in its safe storage place.

What he didn't realize was that one of the caps had fallen on the floor during the transaction.

Mollie, who was in the early stages of her fifth pregnancy, was busy preparing breakfast and getting Beatrice and Elsie Mae ready for school. That done, she began sweeping the living room floor, unaware of the small object that her broom was pushing toward the fireplace.

Raymond Gardner in 1910

Her two-year-old son, Raymond, born after their move to Grabtown, was standing by the blazing fire when she swept the stray dynamite cap into the fireplace. The explosion thrust flaming spears of firewood into Raymond's abdomen.

The child was taken over

eight miles of rutted, muddy road to the hospital in Smithfield, but efforts to save him were futile. He died on February 21, 1911.

The sorrow that gripped the family was magnified by guilt for Mollie and Jonas.

If only the dynamite cap had not been dropped.... If only someone had spotted it on the floor.... If only....

Raymond was buried in Wilson County in a small, secluded cemetery belonging to his mother's family near the Pitt County line. On the grave was placed a winged cherub writing the name RAYMOND on a long scroll. On the back base of the stone was a verse:

> *A loved one from us is gone*
> *A voice we loved is stilled*
> *A place is vacant in our home*
> *Which never can be filled*

Less than seven months after Raymond's death, on September 11, 1911, Mollie gave birth to another son, Jonas Melvin Gardner. Called Melvin early on, he later would be known by his nickname, Jack.

By the time Mollie gave birth to another child, her fourth daughter, Myra Merritt Gardner, on November 5, 1915, the family had begun to fall on hard times.

Farming was always a risky and back-breaking venture, dependent on weather and many other uncontrollable factors. Farmers worked long and hard, and all too often to no gain. So it was for Jonas and his brother, Ben. Bad season fell upon bad season. Then came the boll weevil, which destroyed their main cash crop, cotton. Years before the 1929 stock market crash that heaped the Great Depression full upon America, an agricultural depression had swept the farmlands of the South.

Raymond's tombstome

18

Jonas and his brothers could not pay the debt on their land and lost it. For a time, Jonas continued to farm as a tenant on land that had been his. Later, he worked at the cotton gin in Grabtown, and operated a sawmill and a small store near the two-story house that he managed to keep.

Jonas and Mollie Gardner with their daughters Inez, left, Elsie Mae, center, and son Jack, wearing a dress, in 1913.

Beatrice, 15, (left) and Elsie Mae Gardner, 14, dressed as twins for these 1918 portraits.

Jack Gardner, 8, and Myra, 4, on the back porch of their home at Grabtown.

Room for More

Mollie was thirty-nine in 1922, her husband forty-four. Nearly seven years had passed since the birth of their last child, and they intended to have no more. Both were surprised when Mollie discovered that she was pregnant again.

Their neighbors, Tom and Minnie Capps, who lived across the road, were expecting another child, too. Minnie had become pregnant about the same time as Mollie.

As time passed, it began to appear that both children might be Christmas babies.

Late on the evening of December 23, Dr. Ralph S. Stevens was summoned from his home in Princeton to the Capps' house. At 1:40 on Christmas Eve morning, he ushered into the world Kenneth Dail Capps, the last of Tom's and Minnie's six children.

Doctor Stevens hardly had time to get back home and catch a nap before he was summoned again to Grabtown.

When Mollie Gardner went into labor, seven-year-old Myra and her eleven-year-old brother Jack were sent to a neighbor's home. It was not deemed appropriate for children to be at a birthing. There was also a fear that something might go horribly wrong, and a desire to protect the children from that kind of experience.

Myra's main worry, she recalled many years later, was that Santa Claus would find her absent from home and would leave her nothing under the tree.

Around ten p.m. on Christmas Eve, the seventh child of Jonas and Mollie let out a robust wail—and everyone else breathed a sigh of relief.

The baby was named Ava, for her aunt, Ava Gardner of Wilson County, the youngest of Jonas' five siblings. Aunt Ava was tall, dark-haired and attractive, but unmarried, a spinster who occasionally lived with Jonas and Mollie. In middle-age she would marry an elderly man for whom she was a caregiver. After his death, she would become caregiver for another elderly man and marry him as well. A lifelong Baptist, in later life she would convert to Mormonism and leave her home and all her belongings to the Mormon Church.

Mollie chose Lavenia for the baby's middle name simply because she thought it was pretty and the four syllables flowed nicely from the two in Ava.

The birth certificate would record that Ava Lavenia Gardner was born in Pine Level, because the family's mail was routed through the Pine Level post office. (Their address would later be changed to Route 2, Smithfield.)

Ava walked and talked early, although she was not nearly so precocious at growing hair. Her sister Myra thought she was never going to have any hair, and Ava would be two before some serious blonde wisps began to emerge.

The child had a rambunctious and adventurous spirit from the beginning. One warm day she climbed to the second floor of the house and wandered into a room where a tall window had been left open. She crawled through the window and onto the porch roof, where she was spotted toddling around by James Capps, a teenaged son

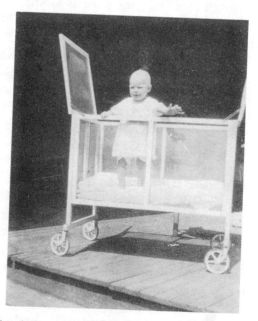

Ava in her crib on the porch at Grabtown. The flaps were lowered to protect her from insects.

of the across-the-road neighbors.

James ran to the house, arriving as Mollie appeared, panic stricken, at the window and began trying to talk Ava back into the house. James stationed himself beneath Ava to catch her if she fell. Ava paid little attention to her mother's pleadings until James remembered that she was fond of peaches. He coaxed her back to the window with a promise that her mother would give her a bowl of peaches and cream.

It would not be the last time that one of the Capps family would come to Ava's rescue.

The Gardner home at Grabtown in the 1920s.
Identity of the young women is unknown.

Moving on Down the Road

Smoking was common in an area where tobacco was a major crop, and most boys were drawn to its pleasures young. Jack Gardner was no exception.

His parents had forbidden him to smoke, but one day when he was thirteen, he slipped into the seed barn by the Grabtown Cotton Gin, closed the door, put an illicit cigarette to his lips, struck a match—and nearly killed himself.

The flame ignited the cotton dust in the air, and the explosion almost blew Jack out of the building. The fire was spectacular. It took down several outbuildings as well as the seed barn, but didn't do critical damage to the gin. Frightened but not badly injured, Jack ran home and hid under a bed.

It is not known if Jonas was held liable for the losses, or whether the fire had anything to do with his family leaving Grabtown. But shortly afterward, in 1925, Jonas and Mollie went before the Johnston County Board of Education with a special request. And the family soon left their home and moved a mile down the road into the old Brogden School, which had been converted into the Teacherage, a boarding house for teachers at the new school next door.

The new school was a two-story brick structure that served grades one through seven. On the first floor was an auditorium with a full stage and seating for 200. No more did the students of the community have to produce their amateur shows on temporary stages with bed sheets for curtains. Students and church groups had a fine place for all kinds of programs. Even country music

Brogden School and its teacherage (left) in the early 1930s.

performers such as Earl Scruggs came to Brogden to put on shows in the new auditorium.

In the 1920s, teachers in public schools in rural North Carolina had to be single females of sterling character, and they were required to live near the schools in which they taught. In the Brogden Teacherage, six teachers lived on the right side of the house. The kitchen, parlor and dining room were in the central area, and the Gardner family lived on the left side. A porch stretched across the front.

Mollie Gardner prepared the meals for the teachers, and Jonas tended the grounds, did repairs as needed, and fired the coal stoves on chilly mornings. Jonas also worked at a sawmill behind the school and continued to farm on a limited basis.

In this new setting Mollie became far more than a cook and the woman in charge of the boarding house. She became a mentor and second mother to the young women who stood at the head of the Brogden classrooms. They called her Mama Gardner.

"Mama Gardner was wonderful in every way, and we all loved her," recalled Susie Cannon, who was a teenager when she began teaching at Brogden School.

The teachers went to the boarding house for lunch during school days, and they looked forward to Mama Gardner's magnificent southern cooking. They were especially fond of a pie that she sometimes served with the noon meal. This palate-pleaser had a layer of vanilla pudding topped with a crust. On top of that was a layer of chocolate pudding. Topping the chocolate layer was a mound of fresh whipped cream enhanced with a tantalizing touch of brandy.

After partaking of such a dessert, the teachers had a little trouble focusing on their classroom duties in the afternoon.

The teachers' boyfriends courted them in the boarding house parlor on Saturday nights and Sunday afternoons, and Ava often would peek from behind the French doors leading to the dining area to see if some bold fellow might be trying to steal a kiss. She also would entertain the visitors with lively dances and acrobatics that seemed to be as natural for her as skipping barefoot down the dusty road. From the beginning, she was tomboy to the bone.

Among the young men who did their courting in the Brogden Teacherage parlor were Theron Johnson of Smithfield, who won the hand of Susie Cannon; and Lyndon Kirkman Jordan, also of Smithfield, who made teacher Rachel Hazelton his bride.

It is not known if Theron and Lyndon were at the Teacherage on a certain day during one holiday season. But some men were on hand to get Jack out of trouble again.

A Christmas tree that reached all the way to the twelve-foot-high ceiling stood in the Teacherage parlor. Like the Christmas trees at the Gardner house in Grabtown, this one was adorned with strings of popcorn, balls of cotton and real candles to be lighted on Christmas Eve.

Jack apparently hadn't learned his lesson about small flames and cotton. He struck a match while standing near the tree. A cotton ball caught fire and the whole tree flashed ablaze.

Only swift action by the young men who were on the premises kept it from becoming a yuletide version of the cotton seed barn disaster. They dragged the burning tree into the yard, singeing the hair on their arms, but otherwise suffering no injuries. Only a little damage was done to the parlor. Jack apparently learned his lesson this time. He was never again known to be the cause of a fire.

By the time Jonas and Mollie moved their family to the

Teacherage, two of their children already had left home. Beatrice, the eldest, had been the first to go. When Ava had first tried to pronounce Beatrice it had come out "Bappie." The name stuck. Bappie had taken a job in Smithfield and was boarding at the home of the Rayford Oliver family well before Ava was born. There she had met William I. Godwin, a tall, good-looking, strong-willed young man who attended Wake Forest College and would become a lawyer. They had married in nearby Selma on October 12, 1922, two and a half months before Ava was born. Beatrice was nineteen, William twenty.

Little more than a year later, on December 15, 1923, Ava's sister Elsie Mae had married David Lester Creech in Micro Township. Elsie was nineteen, David twenty-one. Whether by coincidence or design, Elsie Mae's wedding fell on the seventeenth birthday of her sister Inez. David Creech was a machinist with Atlantic Coast Line Railroad in Rocky Mount, where he and Elsie Mae set up housekeeping.

Elsie Mae was pregnant when David was laid off from his railroad job a year and a half later, and they came to stay at the

Teacherage, where their first child was born on September 28, 1925. The baby was named David Allison Creech, in honor of his father and his mother's lost brother, Raymond Allison Gardner. He was nicknamed Al.

Ava was not quite three when the baby was born, and she hovered over him like a miniature mother, setting a pattern for their relationship throughout their childhood years.

David later got another job with the railroad in

Ava's nephew, Al Creech, over whom she doted as a child.

Tampa, Florida, and moved his family there, but when the job ended after the stock market crash of 1929, he would bring his family back to Brogden and operate a store next to the Teacherage.

When Ava was four-and-a-half, her sister Inez married Smithfield native John Alvis Grimes, called Johnnie, on June 27, 1927. His father served as the Johnston County sheriff for a number of years.

Their vows were spoken before Elder Jesse T. Barnes of the Smithfield Primitive Baptist Church, and the witnesses were Jack Gardner, James T. Capps Jr., and Mrs. Jesse Barnes. One thing was unusual about the ceremony. For reasons now unknown, it took place at six in the morning.

Johnnie Grimes was parts manager for Sanders Motor Company in Raleigh, and he and Inez lived there on Fairview Road.

Ava's sister, Inez Gardner, in her 1927 wedding engagement photo.

By the time of Inez's wedding, Bappie's marriage was beginning to fall apart.

Later, when Bappie announced her intentions to leave her husband it was considered scandalous. In rural North Carolina in the 1920s, divorce was not only rare but considered a personal failing at best, an unforgivable sin at worst.

The Gardner family was Baptist. Jonas sawed the lumber and helped build the original Sardis Baptist Church on Brogden Road, and Mollie had served for a time as the church's Sunday school superintendent. Baptists were almost as strict as Catholics in regard to divorce. Even if married couples were dreadfully unhappy, they were still expected to stick together and plod on through the years, like teams of weary plow horses moving down endless hot and dusty rows.

There had never been a divorce in Bappie's parents' families.

But in spite of the tongues that would be set wagging, Bappie divorced William Godwin and moved to Richmond, Virginia, where she got a job in a clothing store. William continued to speak openly of his love for Bappie, and it would be many years before he married again, a union that would end swiftly. He would remain single for the rest of his life, build an illustrious legal career in Johnston County, and continue a close relationship with the Gardner family.

Bappie eventually would move to New York City, where she would marry again, this time to Larry Tarr, a short, handsome, charming photographer who operated a studio on Fifth Avenue. Many years later, this marriage would prove fateful for Ava.

At 4, Ava (smallest child) was mascot
to Brogden School's 4th grade class.

Banner Brogden Years

By age five, Ava's head was covered with a thick mass of blonde curls, and her face sent one Brogden visitor home to Smithfield to tell his wife, "I just saw the prettiest child I've ever laid eyes on."

Ava's curls were considered to be no asset by her. Having her hair brushed and combed was something she struggled to avoid. Teacher Susie Cannon recalled that Ava's curls would become such a tangled mess that she would scream and yelp, as if being tortured, when her mother or a teacher administered some necessary grooming.

There was nothing prissy about Ava. She had no time for activities that most girls preferred. Her favorite toy was a tobacco stick with a string tied to one end that she pretended to be her horse. She loved running barefoot and keeping pace with the rough-and-tumble farm boys. She also was picking up "cuss words" from them that she didn't dare utter in front of her parents or the teachers, even when they were painfully tugging at her hair with brushes.

Ava's early fascination with heights continued to embolden her. At six, she climbed the water tower behind the school. When she got to the top and looked down, she temporarily lost her nerve and was too frightened to come back down. Ava's across-the-road neighbor in Grabtown, Tom Capps, coaxed her down. The experience didn't quell her adventurous spirit, though.

"In my mind, I can still see Ava going up that water tower," recalled Clarence Woodall, one of the neighborhood boys, who was a few years older than Ava. "She climbed it a lot, not just the time she went too high and lost her nerve."

• • •

One of Ava's favorite playmates was a black boy called Shine, who was about her age. He had run away from home in another part of the state and was staying wherever somebody would take him in. After being beaten at one place, he ran away again and came to Brogden, where Ava's sister and brother-in-law, Elsie Mae and David Creech, prepared a place for him to stay in a small building behind their house. During summer harvest time, he worked with Ava and Al as they handed the huge tobacco leaves to the stringers, who tied them on sticks to be hung in the wood-fired curing barns. He also helped Ava's father at the sawmill behind the school, and if someone was needed to cook chicken or fish, Shine could do it as well as any adult.

After a few years, though, Shine took off for parts unknown, and Ava never saw him again. But he always had a special place in her heart.

Another of Ava's playmates was Marion Grimes, the little sister of her brother-in-law Johnnie, Inez's husband. Marion was only a few months younger than Ava. On Sunday afternoons, Johnnie and Inez would bring her to the Teacherage, and the two girls would play while the grown-ups visited.

Marion was a dainty child, and in later years she said, "I was a little afraid of Ava. There didn't seem to be anything she wouldn't do on a dare."

Marion usually wore her Sunday best, and her mother always cautioned, "Now Marion, don't you get your clothes dirty."

Marion always hoped to please her mother, but her best intentions were for naught when she was with Ava.

"There was a huge sawdust pile behind the school," she recalled, "and as soon as I got to the Teacherage, Ava would drag me to the top of the pile."

There also were mud holes to be sloshed through and tree limbs to be perched on, and Marion never returned home with her clothes in a condition that pleased her mother.

One Christmas, Johnnie and Inez gave Marion and Ava identical celluloid dolls with arms and legs that moved. "I was thrilled with mine," Marion said, "but Ava didn't seem to care much about hers."

• • •

Ava at 5, served as flower girl for the wedding of teacher Rachel Hazelton and Lyndon K. Jordan

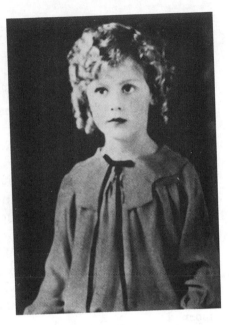

Only on very special occasions was Ava persuaded to rein in her tomboyish ways. One of those times was on March 24, 1928, when teacher Rachel Hazelton became the bride of Lyndon K. Jordan.

The wedding took place in Smithfield and Ava was the flower girl. She wore a long-sleeved dress that her mother had made, long stockings, and high-buttoned shoes. Her hair hung in perfect ringlets.

Ava even sat still for studio portraits. For one profile pose, she gazed at a long-stemmed rose in her hand. For another, she looked almost straight into the camera with no hint of a smile, as if to say, "Is this ever going to end?"

It was around this time that teacher Susie Cannon treated Ava to her first train ride. The two went to Susie's hometown of Hertford, N.C. for a weekend visit with her family.

"Ava was the sweetest little thing," Susie recalled. "All my relatives loved her."

When Ava entered first grade in the fall of 1928, her teacher was a soft-spoken young woman named Maggie Williams.

In one respect, Maggie was different from the other teachers who lived in the boarding house. The other teachers were single, as the school board rules required, but Maggie was married. Why was she allowed to teach and live at the Teacherage?

An exception was made because her husband, David Marshall Williams, was in prison. He was serving time for fatally shooting a law officer who had been on the verge of raiding his liquor still in a nearby county.

Some believed the fatal shot came from another man's gun, but that could not be proven in court.

It would be some time before anyone realized there was something else about Maggie's husband that could be spoken about with comfort—and eventually with pride.

While Maggie was teaching Ava to read and write, her husband was finishing his last year in prison and putting final touches on his design for a new type of carbine rifle. After being released in 1929, Williams, who would become widely known by the nickname Carbine, took his invention to the Winchester Company, which eventually began production of the rifle.

The carbine would become a favorite weapon among U.S. troops in World War II, when millions of them were made, making David Marshall Williams a very rich man. He later would have his own experience with Hollywood and Ava would be there when it happened.

In her declining years, and alone after her husband's death at age seventy-five, Maggie Williams still fondly remembered Ava. She behaved well in class, she said, and earned good marks.

Ava's best friend during her years at Brogden was Clara Whitley, who stored up vivid memories of their days together.

"Children learned responsibility back then," recalled Clara. "Ava was not allowed to play during school recess until she went to the Teacherage and carried in the firewood and coal that her mother needed. And I usually helped her with that chore."

At lunchtime, Clara ate at the boarding house with Ava. "But we didn't want to sit in the dining room with the teachers," she recalled. "We sat on the firewood box by the kitchen stove."

To Clara, it seemed that Mollie was seldom away from the Teacherage kitchen.

"Ava's mother would come out of the house on Friday afternoons and watch the children play on the sawdust pile and get on the school buses," she said.

Because Ava lived next to the school, it was a special treat for her to ride the school bus home with Clara now and then to spend the night.

Ava enjoyed eating at Clara's house as much as Clara enjoyed eating at the Teacherage. Like Mollie, Clara's mother, Zilphia Daughtry Whitley, was a grand Southern cook who served the girls ham, grits, biscuits, and homemade syrup for breakfast.

"Ava liked to pour the syrup over her biscuits," Clara recalled. "She had a bad habit of chewing her fingernails down to the quick, and in my mind I can still see her sucking the syrup off those fingers."

If the grand desserts at the Teacherage or the Whitley home didn't satisfy the girls' hunger for sweets, they'd go to the sawmill where Jonas Gardner was busy turning logs into boards.

Clara remembered him as a dark-haired man of medium height, gentle and soft-spoken. "I think Ava inherited her voice from him," she said.

At the sawmill, the two pals would stand by without saying a word until Ava's father paused at his work. "Then, also without saying a word, he'd reach into his overalls pocket and take out two pennies, one for each of us," Clara said. "We'd run to David Creech's Store and buy two lollipops."

She recalled that there was a black janitor at Brogden School, and Ava would sometimes run to him and give him a big hug. Sometimes he'd give her a whole dime.

Throughout her life, Ava would be known never to be prejudiced, and to stand up for those who were treated unjustly because of the color of their skin. Clara said she felt those strong feelings had their roots in Brogden, where Ava cared deeply for her black playmate, Shine, and the kind and generous black janitor at her school.

When she was in first grade, Ava gave her first stage performance—as Little Rose in Brogden School's 1929 operetta, *A Rose Dream*.

The show was directed by teacher Lillian Blue, with teacher Ruth Huggins at the upright piano.

Students representing grades one through seven took part in the production, which was about a little girl named Rose who wandered from home, became lost, and fell asleep under a tree.

35

Discovered by fairies, Rose was safely led through the Land of the Lost and on to Fairyland by an elf guide named Hop-o-my-Thumb and a band of roses acting as bodyguards.

According to Lillian Blue's notes on an old copy of the operetta, Edwin Thompson played Hop-o-My-Thumb. Among the other cast members were Esther Mae Creech, Helen Lee Creech, Lucy Olive, Clara Whitley, Ruth Whitley, Esther Mae Allen, and Grace Lee.

After seeing many marvelous sights in Fairyland, Rose became drowsy once more, and the Fairy Queen sent Hop-o-my-Thumb to tell the child's worried mother that she could be found slumbering beneath a lilac tree in the park.

Even the pink, yellow, and red crepe paper petals on the rose bodyguards were beginning to droop by the time the Fairy Queen announced:

A mortal child can never stay
In Fairyland but for a day.

The curtains closed to rousing applause and the audience walked into the spring night feeling proud and thoroughly entertained.

After such a debut, Ava surely was justified in thinking that more plum parts in school productions would come her way—but such was not to be.

Clara recalled that the only time she and Ava had a falling out was over a mix-up about a role in a school Christmas play.

"Ava wanted to be the Christmas Angel," Clara said, "and one day she even left class to rehearse the part."

But she found out that the role had been given to Clara, whose straight blonde hair and blue eyes looked more angelic to the teacher in charge than Ava's curly top and hazel eyes.

This caused the two girls to claim other best friends for a time, but they soon picked up where they left off.

There would, however, come a time when both Ava and Clara auditioned for the same role in another production, and Ava would lose again. A teacher stood at the back of the auditorium and listened to the girls read for the part of Betsy Ross. Clara's voice carried well, she decided, but Ava's was too soft to be heard beyond the first rows.

Ava took her loss in stride and later wrote in Clara's autograph book:

Roses may wither
Stems may die
Friends may forsake you
But never will I.

In a little less poetic expression of affection, she wrote:

Rickety Rackety Rust
I'm not allowed to cuss
But damn it to hell
I love you so well
I'm just about to bust.

Ava was eight when her sister Elsie Mae and her family returned to Brogden to stay. Her cousin Al was five, and she immediately took him under wing.

"Ava was always very protective of me," he recalled. The other boys knew if they picked on Al, they'd have to answer to Ava, and few wanted to risk that.

"If I played marbles with the boys and lost all mine, Ava would get into a later game and win every one of them back for me," Al said.

Clarence Woodall well remembered her expertise at that game.

"I played marbles with her many a time," he recalled when in his eighties. "We'd get down in the dirt and draw a circle and try to knock each other's marbles out of the ring. If Ava got vexed with any of us, she'd pinch us on the arm."

One of the Brogden teachers, Ruth Huggins, owned a Model-

A Ford, and she would take Mama Gardner, Ava, and some of the teachers for occasional joy rides.

In the early days of the Depression, folks had little or no money and were losing jobs, houses, and land. In such desperate times, they sought strength and comfort through close bonds with family and friends, and found hope and faith in the many little churches that dotted the countryside.

Whenever they could afford it, they found escape in the movies shown at the Howell Theater in Smithfield. C.E. Howell, the theater owner, purchased a bus on credit and sent it into the countryside to pick up customers. But Ava and her mother had their own transportation in Ruth Huggins' Model-A.

Ruth would recall a day in 1932, when Ava was nine, and she drove Ava and her mother to the Howell Theater to see Mama Gardner's favorite actor, Clark Gable, and the "blonde bombshell," Jean Harlow, in *Red Dust*. A story of love and adventure set in Africa, it was the kind of film that could make a nine-year-old girl long to become a movie star like Harlow, whose earthy character,

Ava's sixth grade class. Ava is at far left on first full row.
Her friend Clara Whitley is at far right on same row.

Honey-Bear Kelly, won the heart of Gable's character, Victor Marsden, safari guide and hunter.

By the sixth grade, Ava and other girls in her class were beginning to look at boys as more than opponents to be clobbered at softball or marble shooting.

Ava's first crush was on schoolmate Luther Daughtry.

Clara recalled that Ava spent the weekend with her at a time when neither of them were in need of a bra. But Ava put on one that belonged to Clara's older sister, Rachel, and wore it to visit one of their neighbors.

One night, while Clara sat beside Ava during a revival service at Sardis Baptist Church, Ava pulled up her skirt to give Clara a glimpse of her new silk panties. The girls were accustomed to having plain cotton underwear, so it was quite a milestone to step into a pair of silky drawers.

Ava had several pairs of shoes, but her new view of boys did not take away her desire to go barefoot at every opportunity. She owned a pair of tennis shoes, but one of the Brogden boys got a lot more use out of them than she did. She loaned them to Ralph Davis, who wore them during baseball games.

39

A Metamorphosis

Neither Ava nor Clara was prepared for the news that hit them in the fall of 1934, when they were in the seventh grade.

Clara remembered that it was on a moonlit night that Ava told her that she and her parents were moving away. They were going to Newport News, Virginia, where Jonas and Mollie would operate a boarding house for shipyard workers.

The Brogden School Teacherage had become a victim of the Depression and the Johnston County Board of Education's lack of funds.

"My heart was broken," Clara said.

The Gardners stayed with Elsie Mac and David Creech for a brief time, and before Christmas, Ava and her mother moved into the boarding house at 3012 West Avenue in Newport News. Jonas stayed on in Brogden for a while to complete his commitment at the sawmill, then joined his wife and daughter in Virginia. (There was never a marital split, as reported in later years.)

Ava presented Clara a good-bye gift before she left.

"She gave me a ten-cent string of pearls and a little snapshot of her sitting on the doorstep at the Teacherage washing her feet before bedtime," Clara remembered.

For a tomboy poised on the edge of turbulent adolescence, leaving the place and the people she loved was difficult.

Facing a classroom of strangers in a new school in the middle of seventh grade wasn't easy either. On the first day, Ava's teacher asked her to stand and tell her classmates her name. They laughed when they heard her country drawl.

But the feeling of not belonging soon faded, and although Ava kept her accent, she made many new friends in Newport News.

During summer vacation, she was allowed to return to North Carolina and spend time with her sisters, Elsie Mae in Brogden, and Inez in Raleigh. She also took the bus to visit her sister Myra, who at twenty had married Bronnie Pearce, from Goldsboro, and moved to Washington, D.C. From there, Ava went on to New York to stay for a while with Bappie.

Clara recalled that she saw her friend during her visit with Elsie Mae the first summer. "I had a new umbrella, and I took it to Elsie Mae's house to show Ava," she said.

Elsie Mae was in the midst of all-out house cleaning, so she fed the girls pork and beans out of a can, peanut butter and crackers, and tea for lunch. "That didn't satisfy us, so we went behind the school and ate a bait of plums," Clara said. "Ava spent the night with me, and some of our schoolmates came the next day and we played in the grove at the school."

Ava and Clara wrote to each other often, but at that time Clara didn't see any reason to save Ava's letters.

Only one letter, from Ava's second summer in Virginia, was found many years later by Clara's mother during spring cleaning.

Ava at 12.

The original is too fragile to reproduce, but Ava's words are as follows, with no changes in spelling and punctuation.

June 4, 1936

Dear Clara,

How is everything at home getting along.
I am going down there the 1st of July but I can't go as early as I did last summer. It certainly is raining hard here. I hope you all are getting it too. Elsia Mae and Inez were here last Sunday & they told me that it was so

dry that they hadn't even set out very much tobacco. It always is too dry or too wet every year.

I saw your name in the paper the other day. Your's & Hellen Lee's & Rubin's. I see that you are just as smart as you every were & I'm just as dumb.

My school will be out tomorrow and I'll be so glad I won't know what to do.

I took all my examinations this week and passed all of them. I know you passed every thing didn't you? I hate school more every day & to think I've got three more years to go.

Do you still want to be a teacher? I know we used to talk about what we wanted to be and you always wanted to be a teacher & me a movie star. I still do but I know I can't so I have about given up hope. I took dancing lessons for about a month & a half but I stoped. I think I'm going to start again soon.

I dreamed about you last night. I guess its because I read your name in the Smithfield Herald. I wish you could come & stay with me this summer. We would go to the beaches & everything. We would have a good time.

Give my love to Rachel. Ask your daddy who the dog has been draging up lately. My dogs are gone now. Boots died the other day & Prince got lost, so I don't have any more.

Are you taking any foreign language? I am taking French & its about to run me crazy, in fact everything I'm taking is because I still hate it all.

Don't it seem funny to say you're going to be in the ninth grade? How do you like to go to school at Princeton? Do you like it as good as Brogden? I don't think high school is much harder than grammar school, do you?

I thought I would go to the dime store & get some ribbon to tie up my hair with but hase'nt stopped rainning yet.

I'm sending you a picture of myself. It's funny looking but they didn't turn out good. Well I guess I'd better stop now and clean up my room.

Please write to me soon & tell me everything about everybody at home. Give my love to your mama. My mama said tell you hello.

You will have to excuse this writing, you'll be doing good to read it, because I can hardly read it myself.

After moving to Virginia at 13, Ava
sent this photo with a letter to her
friend Clara in 1936.

Lots of Love,
Ava

In the photo, the tilt of Ava's head gave a clear hint about a metamorphosis that at age thirteen was in the early stages.

After the summer of 1936, Ava spent less vacation time in Brogden and more at Holt Lake near Smithfield, which was the favorite gathering spot for Johnston County's young people. Her activities were carefully monitored by Elsie Mae and also by her brother Jack, who was one of the most eligible bachelors in the county, a dashing man-about-town who worked in the office of Hooks and Layne Oil Company in Smithfield and lived in the Gabriel Johnston Hotel on South Fourth Street. Ava's parents were always strict, and so were her siblings and other relatives when she

Ava at 14

was in their care.

By the time Ava began going to Holt Lake, the metamorphosis that had shown itself in the photo she sent to Clara was about to turn a gangly tomboy into an astonishing beauty.

M.W. "Mokie" Stancil of Smithfield well remembered when the butterfly was about to emerge from the cocoon. He was two years older than Ava and had a steady girlfriend, Marilyn Coltrane of Smithfield. The two spent many carefree summer days at Holt Lake swimming, boating, and dancing in the pavilion to the recorded music of Glenn Miller, Tommy Dorsey, Benny Goodman, and Artie Shaw.

"A young fellow could dance away a summer evening and not have to spend much more on his girlfriend than the price of a Coca Cola," Mokie remembered.

Ava first went to Holt Lake the summer she was thirteen and didn't draw much attention. But the next summer, dancers came to a standstill when she walked into the pavilion.

"She had long hair, and she wore a yellow shorts and halter outfit," Mokie said. Johnston County boasted many attractive girls, but no one had seen a beauty quite like Ava.

Boys scrambled to attract her attention, and Mokie later admitted he wouldn't have minded dating her himself. "I knew if I asked Ava out it would be the end of me and Marilyn," he said, "and I didn't want that to happen." Besides, he knew that Ava wouldn't date a guy with a steady girl.

Ava was cautious about the boys who asked her out and turned to Mokie, a trusted friend, for guidance. For a time, anybody who wanted a date with Ava had to put in a request through Mokie. If

Ava's friend Mokie Stancil screened her dates at Holt Lake.

Mokie said he was nice, Ava would say, "Okay, I'll go out with him—but only if you go with us."

At this point, Ava had become extremely shy, and Mokie remembered that when he and Marilyn double dated with Ava and Bennett Creech of Selma, Ava rarely spoke, making for hardly any conversation.

"He was as bashful as she was," Mokie said. (Bennett went on to become a noted cardiologist.)

When Ava returned to stay with Elsie Mae the following year, at fifteen, she faced a veritable army of suitors. Some of her dates were approved by Mokie, some arranged by her second cousin, Fred Gardner of Smithfield.

Burton "Bubsy" Sugg of Smithfield recalled that his pal Fred Gardner asked him to escort his cousin to a dance at the American Legion building in Smithfield. Fred was a football hero at Smithfield High and later would go on to greater glory as a member of the "Wolfpack" team at North Carolina State University in Raleigh.

Bubsy wanted to accommodate his friend, but he wasn't keen on the notion of a blind date. "Well...I don't know," Bubsy recalled telling Fred. "What does your cousin look like?"

"She's right pretty," Fred replied.

On the evening of the big dance, Bubsy could hardly believe his eyes, and Ava told friends she could hardly take hers off Bubsy's.

Years later, friends reported that Ava still talked about Bubsy Sugg's "blue, blue eyes," but Bubsy said he couldn't believe she said such a thing. He thought she couldn't have had time to even notice the color of his eyes, because the other fellows at the shindig barely gave him a chance to dance with her.

That turned out to be Bubsy's only date with Fred's cousin.

Almost Like Going Home

Two years after moving to Newport News, Jonas Gardner's health began to decline. He had serious respiratory problems and developed a cough that wouldn't go away.

On March 26, 1938, Ava's gentle, soft-spoken, and beloved father died in Riverside Hospital. His body was returned to Smithfield, where a graveside service was conducted in Sunset Memorial Park by Rev. C.E. Gillespie, pastor of First Baptist Church. Among the survivors were Jonas' brother, Charles Gardner, and his sister, Mrs. M. M. Ware of Raleigh, the aunt for whom Ava was named.

After the funeral, Ava and her mother returned to the boarding house in Newport News and tried to adjust to life without Jonas. Even with the loving support of family and friends, it was a difficult time, and decisions about their future had to be made.

Meanwhile, in the rural community of Rock Ridge in Wilson County, N.C., school officials found themselves without a qualified person to operate their boarding house for teachers.

Varneda Woodard, who had taught at Brogden before coming to Rock Ridge, came up with the idea of persuading Mama Gardner to take the job. Mollie and Ava came to Rock Ridge that summer to look the place over and liked what they saw.

They moved in August, and both were delighted to be back in North Carolina and closer to family.

Rock Ridge was a small, closely-knit farm community some thirty-five miles from Brogden. The name came from a two-story brick school built in 1883 on a rocky rise. It was first called Rocky Ridge, but some residents wanted to drop the "y." A meeting was held, a vote taken, and Rocky was chipped down to Rock.

The original school building, erected the year Mollie was born, was still in use when Mollie and Ava moved there. It served grades one through eleven, and students who attended outlying grammar schools usually transferred to Rock Ridge in the sixth grade. (Grade twelve would not be added to public schools until later.)

Among the first people Mollie and Ava met at Rock Ridge were Emily Sheffield, a young fourth grade teacher who was expecting her first child and had taken leave from the classroom; and Emily's husband, Dewey, who taught high school vocational agriculture. They lived in an apartment on the first floor of the Teacherage, a two-story clapboard house with a front porch, and Mollie and Ava lived in an apartment on the other side of the first floor. Several single female teachers lived on the second floor.

Although Emily was in her mid-twenties and nearer Ava's age than Mollie's, she and Mollie became the closest of friends. Each weekday around ten, Mollie would walk down the steps at her kitchen door, traipse around the house and up the steps to Emily's kitchen, or Emily would make the same trip in reverse. The two would sit at the table, drink Coca Cola, and talk.

"We enjoyed that so much," Emily recalled years later.

As at the Brogden Teacherage, Mollie became the beloved "second mother" to the teachers, and as before, they called her Mama Gardner.

Emily recalled that Mollie and Ava brought a living room suite and bedroom suite to Rock Ridge, and Ava also brought beautiful clothes that her mother had made or that had been given to her by siblings.

As the days went by, it became clear to Emily that the Gardners were a loving and devoted family

Ava with Dewey Sheffield Jr., whom she babysat, at Rock Ridge.

and that Mollie and Ava missed Jonas very much. Once during their morning visit in the kitchen, Mollie told Emily, "I wish I could dream about my husband. I dream almost every night, but I've never had a dream about Jonas."

After living in Newport News for three and a half years, Ava once again faced the prospect of making new friends. Alberta Cooney was the first classmate she met on the first day of her senior year at Rock Ridge School on October 1, 1938.

One of the teachers, Louise Tunstall, took Alberta by the hand and asked if she would show a new girl around and introduce her to other students.

Louise lived in the Teacherage, and she may have been aware that Alberta and Ava had a lot in common.

Most obvious were their looks. Both had fair skin and dark hair, with Ava's having auburn tones that became prominent in sunlight. Both girls had the kind of hazel eyes that could act as chameleons and appear to be green or blue or brown, depending on their surroundings and the color of their clothing.

"I thought Ava was the prettiest girl I'd ever seen," Alberta recalled of their first meeting. But something else also struck her about Ava.

"Her voice was so deep and husky that everybody thought she had a cold or laryngitis, but we soon learned it was her natural voice."

But more important, both girls had lost their fathers. Alberta's father, Frank Cooney, died of a rare blood disorder when she was thirteen. Her mother, the former Bertha Raper, later married Jim Hinnant, who treated Alberta as his own daughter.

Ava and Alberta didn't talk much about their fathers, perhaps because Ava's loss was too fresh and the pain too profound to be put into words.

Alberta, Ava, and another classmate, Margie Williamson, soon became close friends, and were known as The Three Musketeers. Right away, Ava wanted to spend the night with her new chums, and at first Alberta was apprehensive about letting her.

She knew that the Teacherage had indoor plumbing and a bathroom, but her own house in the Spring Hill Township eight miles from Rock Ridge didn't.

However, Alberta soon learned that Ava was just as comfortable at the wash basin and in the outhouse as she would have been in a millionaire's gold-fixtured bathroom.

She was so comfortable, in fact, that when Ava was in the outhouse and heard Alberta's stepfather drive into the yard in his A-Model Ford, she would open the door a tad and call a greeting, "Hey Jim!," then quickly shut the door.

"She managed to do that without revealing a thing," Alberta recalled. "My mother thought it was so funny."

The road in front of Alberta's house was unpaved, and Ava loved to walk barefoot on the road and feel the cool, smooth tire tracks beneath her feet. As soon as she arrived at the Hinnant home, she kicked off her shoes and put them in the mailbox by the road.

Alberta recalled that Ava had one pair of shoes that she never wore. They were green, and they sat atop a chiffonrobe in her bedroom.

Ava explained that they were a gift from her sister Bappie, and that they had once belonged to film star Irene Dunn.

Another thing Ava wanted to do as soon as she arrived at Alberta's was to visit Alberta's cousins, two-year-old James Raper and his baby sister Mel Frances, who lived just down the road.

"It was no big deal to me, because I saw the children all the time," Alberta said. "But Ava loved to hold the baby and get down on the floor and play with James."

As a small child, Alberta danced her way to first place in numerous talent contests, and when Rock Ridge High organized a band, she was chosen as one of the first majorettes.

"The majorettes made their hats out of construction paper and painted them gold," she said. "We wore saddle oxfords and a woman at Rock Ridge made our white outfits trimmed in the school colors of blue and gold. We made our batons out of broomsticks."

The band was an exciting addition to Rock Ridge, but Ava showed no interest in becoming a majorette or playing an instrument. (There were no cheerleaders at the school then.)

Academically, Ava was an average student. But Alberta remembered one class session when her friend demonstrated ability well above the rest. No plays were presented in Ava's senior year, but there was a literature class. One day the teacher assigned each student a part in a play and asked them to read it aloud.

"I don't remember the name of the play," Alberta said, "but I do remember that Ava read her part better than anyone. She put some meaning and emphasis in it, while everyone else just said the words."

Alberta recalled that Ava "could get very excited about everything." That enthusiasm was apparent one night in their senior year when Ava paid a visit to the Hinnant home. The house was dark and everyone was asleep when Alberta was awakened by the sound of pebbles hitting her bedroom window and someone calling her name.

"I knew it was Ava," she said, "because that husky voice said 'Alberta' like nobody else could."

She put on a housecoat and went to the front porch, where Ava was waiting with a young man. They didn't tarry long, and Alberta doesn't recall the name of Ava's companion that night, but before she went back to his car, she whispered to Alberta, "When I get married, I'm going to marry someone from Smithfield."

Ava's sister Inez had been a star on the girls basketball team at Princeton High School in Johnston County, and sister Myra and brother Jack also excelled in sports there. But even though Ava's tomboyishness and acrobatic skills extended into her high school years, and far beyond, she was only once briefly involved in sports.

That happened at a basketball game when Rock Ridge was unable to come up with substitute players and Ava volunteered. In those days girls' basketball was played under half-court rules. But when a team member threw the ball to Ava, she headed to the goal on the wrong end of the court. Mingled with the sound of the ball's rapid thump-thump-thump was the laughter of the spectators.

Not only did she go to the wrong goal, Alberta remembered, she missed the shot when she got there.

Usually she and Ava didn't talk much about boys, Alberta recalled, and they never gossiped about other girls at Rock Ridge. But they found plenty of things to talk about and giggled a lot. "We just had the most fun anyone can imagine," Alberta said.

Once they visited a fortune teller, Madam Bogart, who had a large sign in front of her dwelling on Highway 301 near Wilson. The only memorable prediction that Madam Bogart gave was that Ava would "go across the great waters."

Ava and Alberta were a mutual admiration society. Ava would tell Alberta, "I love your eyes," and Alberta would tell Ava, "I wish I had your hair."

Now and then when they spent the night with each other, Alberta would stare at Ava while she was sleeping and wonder how any girl could look so perfect.

"Her beauty was natural," she said. "I wore makeup, but all Ava wore was a very light touch of lipstick." The brand Tangee was popular with young girls of that era, and could be bought at any dime store for a modest price. Cutex fingernail polish was also within the financial range of Rock Ridge girls, and Ava enjoyed painting her nails over and over.

"She had a habit of peeling off her nail polish the day after she put it on," Alberta said. "And sometimes she'd put her hand on my desk at school and tell me to peel it off for her."

One thing Ava loved about visiting Alberta was that on Sunday afternoons her stepfather was apt to proclaim, "You girls come on, and I'll take you to a movie." Away they would go in the Model-A Ford, which seemed to whisk them like a golden chariot to the enchanted theater in Wilson.

For Alberta the nights she spent with Ava in the teacherage became treasured memories.

"Ava's mother was the sweetest, most wonderful woman," she said. "She often made a delicious chocolate cake, and would always send word for me to come and have a piece. She told me she put grated potatoes in the cake, but I don't know if she meant the batter or the icing."

In Ava's home, "I love you" was said freely and often. "I knew that my parents loved me," Alberta said, "but it was just not their nature to say so."

When it came time for Ava and Alberta to go to bed, Mollie always tucked them in and gave each a goodnight kiss.

"This was amazing to me," Alberta said.

While Ava didn't talk about her father, she did speak often about her brother Jack, and it was obvious that she adored him. Emily Sheffield recalled that Jack came to Rock Ridge every weekend and gave his mother part of his paycheck.

During this period, he opened Jack's Grill inside a Texaco service station leased by Hooks and Lane Oil Company on Highway 301 in Wilson County, a few miles beyond the Johnston County line, and Ava loved going there.

When December of 1938 rolled around, Ava was becoming excited about the impending birth of the Sheffields' baby. She also was looking forward to blowing out sixteen candles on her birthday cake on Christmas Eve.

But before either event took place, calamity struck the community. Rock Ridge School was destroyed by fire on December 4.

After the fire, some classes were held in the school gym, which survived the blaze, others in a nearby church. It was not the kind of year that Rock Ridge seniors had envisioned. But for Ava, the excitement and dismay brought by the fire soon was replaced by new excitement.

Emily's first child, Dewey Bain Sheffield Jr., was born just fifteen days after the fire, and Ava was thrilled to have a baby so close at hand. As soon as she came home from school, she'd go to the kitchen, get something to eat, and head to the Sheffields' apartment to play with the baby.

"Ava was never little Dewey's paid sitter," Emily said. "She did spend a lot of time with him, just because that's what she wanted to do. She adored him, and we all adored her."

Dewey Sheffield owned one of the few cars parked at the Teacherage, and when his wife and Mollie needed to go shopping or run errands, he would serve as driver.

One day when they were heading to a grocery store in Wilson, Mollie commented, "I thought it would be a long time before we'd get to go anywhere, but it's only been three weeks and here we are going again!"

In his role as a vocational agriculture teacher, Dewey went to N.C. State University several times a year, and Emily, the baby, Mollie, and Ava would sometimes ride along.

One day, while Ava was in school, Emily and Mollie took the trip and visited the N.C. State Library. Mollie was carrying

Dewey when they approached the steps to the second level, where the restrooms were.

"Emily, I think you'd better take the baby," Mollie said. "I'm afraid my knee might give out on me."

Emily took Dewey and had gone part way up the stairs when she looked back and saw that Mollie had fallen.

"She wasn't all sprawled out," she explained. "She was just down on her knees, but that was bad enough in front of all those college students."

When she and several students rushed to help, they saw that Mollie was laughing. And when they all realized that she wasn't injured, they had a good laugh too. "She had a great sense of humor," Emily said.

As the chill of Tar Heel winter was swept away by blossoms of early spring, plans were made for the most anticipated events of the school year—the junior-senior banquet and commencement exercises.

Another special activity was reserved only for seniors: picking the 1938-39 Class Superlatives.

When the vote was taken for Most Beautiful, Ava and Alberta tied. Both were sent out of the room while their classmates wrestled with the dilemma. Two girls simply couldn't be Most Beautiful.

The solution they came up with was to name Ava Prettiest, and Alberta Most Attractive.

Since neither Ava, Alberta, or Margie, had dated any Rock Ridge boys, it was perhaps no surprise that they ended up without escorts on the night of the junior-senior banquet.

The banquet was the equivalent of a senior prom, but without dancing. (Proms would not be held in the area's high school until many years later.) For banquet night, girls donned evening gowns and hoped they looked so pretty that they'd soon be dressed as brides.

Boys wore dark suits and white shirts, and hoped they looked like young men, rather than mere boys having their oxygen supply reduced by their neckties.

The seniors were especially thrilled that for the first time the banquet would not be held in the school lunchroom. Because of the fire, the event would unfold in a place with real class—the Cherry Hotel in Wilson.

Ava rode to the banquet with classmate Ruby Williamson Barnes, but years later Ruby couldn't recall who drove or what Ava wore. "I do remember she fretted because she had washed her hair and it was still wet," Ruby said.

Although Ava, Alberta, and Margie were dateless, they were not without male companionship that night. Seated at their table was the Rev. John Barclay, pastor of Wilson's First Christian Church, who several days later delivered the baccalaureate sermon at Rock Ridge.

Having a preacher at their table didn't cause the Three Musketeers to have any less fun. Rev. Barclay had a grand sense of humor and their table not only erupted regularly with giggles but also roared with hearty laughter.

Ava did get to attend a high school prom that spring, after all, at least briefly. Walter F. Lewis lived with his parents in a small duplex apartment next door to Ava's sister Inez in Raleigh. He met Ava when she visited her sister shortly after moving back to North Carolina.

He remembered that Ava was polite, reserved, and unaffected by her natural beauty. "She handled her good looks well, never turning to see who might be staring at her," he said, "and I can vouch for the fact that when we were together all eyes were not on me."

When he learned that Ava had no transportation to visit Inez, he offered to drive to Rock Ridge and bring her anytime she wanted to visit, and she took him up on it several times.

"I was confident that she was as glad to see me as I was to see her," Walter remembered, "and that misconception went on for months."

That fall, Walter took Ava to the State Fair under the assumption that the admission was free on Fridays. When they got to the entrance, he was dismayed to learn that admission was seventy-five cents. "I only had three dollars, so we walked around back and crawled under a fence," he said. "In those days, three dollars was enough to have a good time at the Fair."

The following spring, Walter invited Ava to attend his junior-senior prom at Broughton High School, and she accepted. They arrived to find the entrance guarded by a teacher who told them the dance was for Broughton students only. No guests allowed.

With nothing else to do, the outcasts found a bicycle outside the building. Ava climbed on the handlebars and Walter pedaled her around the grounds. When they came to a steep embankment, Ava insisted on going down it. "And we made it!" Walter said. "She was a real sport."

Later, they sneaked in a side door in time to enjoy a few dances. Jimmy Allen, who played the piano that night, remembered how popular Ava was and how often the other Broughton fellows cut in on Walter.

Ava's graduation exercises were held on a hot afternoon on the Rock Ridge ballfield. "It was the prettiest graduation Rock Ridge ever had," Emily Sheffield recalled.

It was also the largest group of graduates to date. Proudly clad in navy blue caps and gowns, sixty-two seniors walked forward to receive their diplomas.

Beneath her gown, Ava wore a new dress, a graduation gift from one of her sisters. It had a tan skirt and bodice of multicolored stripes. Later in the day, she wore a wristwatch that was a gift from her brother Jack.

Ava seemed happy to have her high school days behind her. When she posed for a snapshot with a small group of fellow graduates, her diploma was rolled as if she intended to swat flies with it, while others proudly displayed theirs for the camera.

Although Ava had no clear plans for her life after graduation, she did have a busy summer ahead.

Charles Barnes was two years older than Ava, and his sister Betsy was slightly younger. Their parents were among the leaders in the Rock Ridge community, and Charles and his father operated an auto repair business across the road from the Teacherage.

"When I had some idle time, I'd go to the Teacherage and talk to Ava," Charles recalled. "And I always made sure that I had that idle time. Ava was a very nice young lady, and she had the most beautiful hair I've ever seen. Her four sisters were good-looking too."

Charles' family had a car, and he drove Ava and Betsy to wherever they needed or wanted to go. Not long after Ava's graduation he took them to the annual June German in Rocky Mount, a dance with music by a big-name band. The name was derived from the meaning of German as "a dance party," or "a dance in which intricate steps are improvised and intermingled with waltzes."

Many fancy steps were being improvised at the June German, Charles later remembered, but they had little to do with waltzes. And Ava had no lack of partners or expertise in doing the new dances.

Ava also was looking forward to another event soon after graduation. The Rock Ridge home economics teacher was taking younger class members to White Lake for a week, and she had asked Ava and Alberta to go along as chaperons.

They were looking forward to the trip, but when Alberta went to the Teacherage to make plans, Ava started crying. Her sister Inez had made plans for her to spend the same week with her in Raleigh.

"I went on without Ava," Alberta said. "It was a big disappointment for both of us."

Ava also stayed with her sister Elsie Mae in Johnston County that summer. She had become close friends with Alma Kilpatrick, the girlfriend of her cousin, Fred Gardner. It was through Alma that she met St. Clair Pugh, who grew up in Smithfield. St. Clair was a year older than Ava and had just completed his freshman year at the University of North Carolina in Chapel Hill.

Alma's mother, Virginia, operated a boarding house, the Lee House, near the courthouse and Ava often stayed there with Alma.

"My mother and I ate dinner at Mrs. Kilpatrick's boarding house when my father was on the road as a representative for a flour company," St. Clair recalled. "And I got to know Ava then."

Ava also frequented Holt Lake as she had for the past three summers. Rustic cottages could be rented at the lake, and young people held "houseparties" in them that lasted as long as a week. These events were well-chaperoned, with girls staying in one cottage and boys in another.

Ava's first boyfriend, Bob Rose, became a star basketball player at the University of North Carolina at Chapel Hill.

It was during one such houseparty that summer that Ava met Robert "Bob" Rose, who stole her heart for the first time. He was the basketball star at Smithfield High and would go on to become a three-time All-Conference player at the University of North Carolina.

Soon after he and Ava became sweethearts, Bob took a surveying job for the summer and when time for another houseparty rolled around, he asked his friend St. Clair Pugh to look after Ava until he finished work and could join the others at the lake.

"I remember taking Ava out in a canoe," St. Clair said. "She tried to teach me to dance the jitterbug, which I think we called 'the little apple' back then. The record we danced to was Artie Shaw's 'Back Bay Shuffle.'"

Ava had even more excitement in store that summer: a trip to New York to visit her sister Bappie and her husband, photographer Larry Tarr.

Ava wrote to Alberta from New York and reported that she had been laughed at for ordering milk in a restaurant.

As on earlier visits, Larry Tarr wanted her to pose for him and she sat for numerous portraits.

Most of the talk in the entertainment world that year was about the new movie *Gone With The Wind*, starring Clark Gable as Rhett Butler and Vivien Leigh as Scarlet O'Hara. For one of her poses, Ava wore a wide-brimmed straw hat with ribbon ties under the chin, ala Miss Scarlet. Neither she nor her brother-in-law could foresee the effect that photo eventually would have on both of their lives.

Ava with Margie Williamson, who won
a trophy for academic achievement,
on graduation day.

The tallest among this group of Rock Ridge High
School graduates, Ava is fourth from left in first row,
holding her rolled-up diploma. Margie Williamson is
second from left, Alberta Cooney, third from left.

Winds of Change

The news coming from radios was ominous in the fall of 1939. Germany's invasion of Poland in September brought Britain and France into the war against Germany. The country was being assured that U.S. forces would not become involved, but uncertainty reigned.

After returning from her summer travels, Ava remained in Rock Ridge helping her mother at the Teacherage. Alberta returned to Rock Ridge School for a post-graduate business course, then took a job as secretary at Buckhorn Grammar School near her home.

Ava went to Chapel Hill that fall to attend dances with both Bob Rose and St. Clair Pugh. St. Clair later took her to the mid-winter dance weekend in Chapel Hill where the Glen Grey Orchestra was playing. They went with Albert Johnson and Mary Elizabeth Beasley of Smithfield in St. Clair's brother's 1926 Chevrolet. The two girls stayed with a woman named Tankersly in Chapel Hill, who rented rooms during dance weekends.

St. Clair recalled that Ava's stag line was all the way out the door of the Tin Can, the gymnasium where the mid-winter dances were held, and he later learned that she slipped out and saw other guys both nights after he dropped her and Mary Elizabeth off at the rooming house.

"I was just pleased to have been the escort of the belle of the ball," he said.

Ava was also seeing other young men from Smithfield at the time. Wade Talton, a student at Duke University, recalled dating her ten or twelve times.

"She let me kiss her goodnight, but there was no parking or

anything like that," he remembered.

Like most other young women in rural North Carolina, Ava had a strict upbringing, and her friend Mokie Stancil later vouched that guys who dated her soon discovered that she fit into the "nice girl" category and that they had no chance of getting far with her. She also had so many offers that she never had to depend on any one guy.

Wade Talton learned that the hard way. One day when he had a date with Ava, he went to see another girl from Atlanta who was visiting relatives in the Johnston County town of Four Oaks.

"I didn't mean to stay long," he recalled, "but the time just slipped away, and before I knew it I was late for my date with Ava. She wouldn't have anything to do with me after that, but we later became friends again."

Soon another summer had rolled around, and Ava entered a tobacco festival beauty pageant in Tarboro, about fifty miles northeast of Rock Ridge. For the event, her mother made her a beautiful Grecian-style gown that was a perfect complement to her hair and complexion.

On the night of the pageant, she had a date with Steve Hilley, son of the president of Atlantic Christian College in Wilson. They double-dated with one of Steve's friends, Loonis McGlohon, and his girlfriend. At the time, Loonis was a student at East Carolina College in Greenville, who would go on to become one of the great composers and jazz pianists of his time, writing songs for Frank Sinatra, Rosemary Clooney and many others.

Loonis recalled that most of the other beauty contestants wore Southern belle gowns with ballooning skirts similar to what folks were seeing in *Gone With The Wind,* and their hair was in cork-screw curls.

Ava, with her loosely-flowing gown and long dark hair in soft natural waves, was the last to appear on stage. She was contestant number fourteen—and she was stunning.

Something even more stunning came when the judges turned in their score cards and the master of ceremonies announced the winner. It wasn't Ava.

"I couldn't figure it out," Loonis said.

• • •

That fall, Ava's friends from Rock Ridge, Alberta Cooney and Margie Williamson, with whom she'd made up the Three Musketeers, boarded a train for Washington, D.C. to seek their fortunes. They were "decked out like Lady Astor's pet horse," Alberta recalled, she in a red two-piece dress and matching turban, handbag, and shoes, and Margie in a similar outfit in pink. "We wanted to look mature and sophisticated," she remembered.

Waiting for them were waitress jobs at High's Ice Cream Parlor for Alberta and Hotshot's Restaurant for Margie. But both soon moved up, Alberta to a secretarial position with the Government Employees Insurance Company, across from the Capitol, and Margie as secretary for a senator from Ohio.

Ava remained behind. She had decided that she wanted to become a secretary, but she knew that her abilities were not adequate. Emily Sheffield was taking courses at Atlantic Christian College in Wilson to keep her teaching certificate up to date, and she suggested that Ava enroll in secretarial classes as a day student and ride back and forth with her.

Jack agreed to pay her tuition.

After Ava started classes, male students made a point of walking by the door of the typing and shorthand classes to get a glimpse of the new girl.

And while some of the girls were apprehensive about Ava stealing their boyfriends, most couldn't help but like her, because she was so friendly and acted as if she were unaware of how pretty she was.

In February of 1941, Ava returned to Johnston County for the funeral of her sister Inez's infant daughter, Linda Lee Grimes. The child had respiratory problems at birth and lived only a month, never becoming well enough to be brought home from the hospital. Inez and Johnnie had two older children, William, called Billy, who was eight; and Mary Edna, six.

After attending her niece's funeral, Ava went to Brogden to visit her best friend from grammar school. She and Clara Whitley had not seen each other since the summer day when they ate a bait

63

Ava, second from left, at Atlantic Christian College.

of plums and played with their school-mates in the grove at the school on Ava's first visit back from Virginia.

Clara had graduated as valedictorian of her class at Princeton High School, and she wanted to continue her education. "But my parents didn't think it was necessary," she said. Instead, she was working at Rose's Dime Store in Smithfield.

She was in the front yard with her parents when Ava arrived behind the wheel of Jack's car.

"Ava had on a black Chesterfield coat and high heels," Clara recalled. "The wind was blowing her hair, and she was simply beautiful."

After the visit, as Ava drove away, she waved to Clara and called out, "You have to come and spend a weekend with me!"

But Clara never did.

A few years later, Clara married Leon Tyner, who became a prosperous farmer in the Brogden community, and they had two sons.

Thomas M. Banks, called Tommy, was twelve in 1941 and lived near Atlantic Christian College. He and his buddies often rode their bikes on campus and teased the pretty girls. One of their main tar-

Tommy Banks got a kiss from Ava at 12 which would affect the rest of his life. Here he was a teenager.

gets was Ava, who waited for Emily Sheffield to pick her up at a certain spot each afternoon.

One day, as he and his pals had done many times before, Tommy whizzed by Ava and called out, "Hey, Girlfriend!" But this time, he didn't pedal fast enough.

Ava chased him down, pulled him off his bike, and kissed him on the cheek while his buddies hooted. Embarrassing though the episode was, it became an unforgettable and inspiring experience that would impact his life and Ava's in years to come.

In the 1940-41 yearbook of Atlantic Christian College, Ava's photo appeared as a Campus Beauty. But Janie Fitzgerald of Pine Level was chosen Most Beautiful that year. Janie and Winton Odham of Grifton were picked to preside as queen and king of the annual May Day festivities. Members of their court from the Wilson area were Elizabeth Ann Nall and Katherine Wainwright.

The *Wilson Daily Times* reported that the program was shaping up as one of the best ever, with many girls performing "dances which are done by pioneer and modern Americans and our neighbors to the south."

An Indian dance and the Virginia Reel would be followed by a dance representing America's conquest of the West, with cowboys and cowgirls "singing their Yippy-I-O-Ky-Ay." After dances representing South America, patriotic North American children would wind the May Pole.

Ava had a role in the festivities as one of the rope-twirling cowpokes who tamed the West.

Alberta had seen Ava only once while Ava was at Atlantic Christian. She had come from Washington to visit her parents and dropped by the Teacherage. "Ava cocked her leg up on a table and lit a cigarette," Alberta recalled. "I had never seen her smoke, and I was shocked."

That summer Ava went to New York to stay with Bappie, and one day Alberta's mother made her usual trek to the mailbox where Ava used to stash her shoes to go barefoot. She found a postcard Ava had addressed to Alberta and forwarded it on to Washington.

On the card, Ava had hurriedly scrawled something about a man spotting her photo in the window of her brother-in-law's studio in New York. At the man's suggestion her sister and brother-in-law had sent a package of her photos to MGM.

"I thought Ava was just daydreaming about being in the movies, and nothing would come of it," Alberta said. "I threw the postcard away, and have regretted it ever since."

Ava as a cowboy in 1941 May Day
program at Atlantic Christian College.

Part Two

And They Knew Her Then

This portrait of Ava by brother-in-law Larry
Tarr in New York in 1939, started her career.

Duhan Does a Double Take

In St. Clair Pugh's University of North Carolina yearbook a classmate wrote jokingly that he had "discovered" Ava Gardner when he asked a photographer to take her picture for *Carolina* magazine during one of her dance weekend visits to the campus with St. Clair.

That classmate would become famous himself.

He was pollster Lou Harris.

The person who actually could claim to have set in motion Ava's imminent climb to fame was Barnard "Barney" Duhan, a clerk in the legal office of Loews Theatres in New York. He was strolling down Fifth Avenue when he casually glanced at the portraits in the window of the Tarr Photography Studio. One made him pause for a closer look.

It was a sepia tone image of a girl wearing a straw hat with ribbon ties under her chin. She was fresh-faced and glowing with the sweet innocence of youth, a delight to behold. Barney, who was in his twenties, was not above a little subterfuge if it could get him a date with a good looking girl.

He often got the telephone numbers of beautiful girls he didn't know, called them up, mentioned he worked for Loews Inc., of which MGM Studios was a part, tossed out the words "talent scout," and watched the magic work.

He decided to try to get the number of the beautiful girl in the window. He walked into Tarr Studio and used his routine on the receptionist, telling her that MGM might be interested in the girl in the window. Would it be possible to get her name and number? Sorry, said the receptionist, but they didn't give out that kind of information.

Well, said a thwarted Barney, attempting a graceful exit, somebody should send her picture to MGM.

Bappie got excited when her husband called to tell her about the visitor's suggestion. She had long thought that Ava could go places on her looks. She had tried, without success, to get her a modeling job during her annual summer visits to New York.

Bappie also thought that Ava had a nice singing voice, and earlier Larry had introduced Ava to the leader of a small nightclub band and talked to him about giving her an audition as a vocalist. He suggested that she make a recording and send it to him. Larry took Ava to a small recording studio where she sang "Amapola," the only popular song to which she knew all the words, with a pianist accompanying her. Larry sent the recording to the band leader, but nothing came of it.

Larry wanted to move quickly to get Ava's pictures to MGM, and he and Bappie stayed in the studio darkroom all night making copies of his recent portraits. After scrutinizing the shot of Ava in the hat, Bappie decided that Ava needed more eye-catching eyelashes and applied some on the negative.

The next day, Larry took the package of photos to MGM's New York office himself, and Bappie called Ava to give her the exciting news. Ava dismissed the idea. She had gotten very excited when she thought she might become a big-band singer, and had even told friends at Atlantic Christian College about it, only to suffer the embarrassment of seeing nothing come from the demonstration record. She didn't think anything would come from this either.

But Larry did get a call from MGM telling him that if Ava could come to New York, Marvin Schenck, who was in charge of talent, would like to talk with her.

Ava spent the night before she left for New York with her friend Alma Kilpatrick in Smithfield.

Rudolph "Rudy" Howell, son of the owner of the Howell Theater, saw Ava that night, when several young people gathered on the porch of the boarding house. He remembered that she was excited but not really taking the possibilities seriously.

"I'm going to marry the biggest star in Hollywood," Ava told them jokingly and everybody laughed.

Although her friends were well aware of Ava's remarkable beauty, they thought she had little or no chance of making it in Hollywood. After all, she had no experience or training, and the offices of movie moguls faced a constant flood of lovely, talented young women who had taken voice lessons, dance lessons, acting lessons.

What chance did an untrained Johnston County country girl have against such competition?

The bus station was on Second Street in Smithfield, across from the courthouse. Tickets were sold inside Stallings Pharmacy, which was on the corner of Second and Market streets and adjacent to the bus stop.

Pharmacist James L. "Jimmy" Creech, who later operated his own drug store in town, was working at Stallings Pharmacy when Ava came in to purchase her ticket to New York. After buying it, she went outside and sat alone on a bench, Jimmy remembered. Before long, the bus turned off Market Street, its air brakes hissing as it stopped.

Ava climbed on and soon was gone.

Bappie went with Ava for her interview with Marvin Schenck. Ava later recalled that Schenck was very sweet. He handed her a script. She'd never seen one before. He would read the male role, he said, and she the female. They began, and after a few lines, Ava realized that he seemed not to be understanding a word she said. She feared that her heavy Carolina accent had done her in.

Maybe a film test would be better, Schenck suggested, and directed her to appear at a studio on Ninth Avenue the following day. She wore a green print dress that her mother had bought for sixteen dollars, and a pair of high heels that she borrowed from Bappie.

The singer Vaughn Monroe ("Ghostriders in the Sky") was being tested at the same time, and Ava later remembered that his ears stuck out so far that they had to be glued down. She went through her brief test without having to glue any parts. She was told to sit, to stand, to walk across the room, pick up a vase of flowers from a table and bring it back. Then she was asked a few questions: Where was she from? Was she in school? What was she studying?

That was it. And it was enough. She was offered a seven-year contract at fifty dollars a week, a contract the studio could get out of almost at any point it chose. Later, Ava would claim that everybody who got a screen test got the same standard contract, because MGM didn't want any other studio to sign them. Whatever the case, she was on her way to Hollywood.

Bappie was excited and proud, and so was their mother when she got the news. But she didn't want her innocent daughter going alone to Hollywood at the age of eighteen. She would need somebody to look after her, to help her get started.

Bappie volunteered. She tried to talk her husband into going, too, but he didn't want to leave the successful chain of photography studios that his father had started. The decision would mean the end of their marriage, although they remained friends.

California, Here They Come!

Ava didn't seem fazed by what might lie ahead of her, not excited at all, as she and her sister made their way across country by train in August, 1941.

"She didn't act like most teenagers would have under those circumstances," Bappie recalled.

Perhaps that was because Ava still thought that nothing was likely to come from this, and she didn't want to get her hopes up. She would just go along and see what happened.

On their second day in Hollywood, Ava and Bappie toured the MGM studios and ate in the commissary. And something did happen—a meeting Ava was unlikely to forget.

Mickey Rooney was on the set that day, filming *Babes on Broadway* with Judy Garland.

He was in heavy women's makeup and dressed like Carmen Miranda for a song-and-dance segment when he spotted Ava and came over to introduce himself. Despite his ludicrous appearance, Ava was flattered by his attentions.

She and Bappie had rented a small, cheap, furnished apartment, and soon after they returned to it from their studio tour, the phone rang. Mickey was calling to see if Ava would like to have dinner.

Mickey's real name was Joe Yule Jr. He had been in show business since he could walk. His parents had been vaudeville performers. Mickey had begun his movie career at age six. Multitalented, he was also loaded with charm and charisma, and Ava would come to think of him as being as cute as a speckled pup. He was the biggest star in Hollywood at the time. MGM was paying him more that it was shelling out for Clark Gable, who had been such a hit in *Gone With the Wind* just two years earlier.

Mickey had no problem snaring dates with Hollywood beauties, but he ran into a problem with Ava, who at five-feet-six was several inches taller than Mickey. She took Bappie's advice and played hard to get, turning Mickey down a number of times before finally agreeing to a date. He also got a quick education about nice Southern girls: Ava made him keep his hands to himself. This was a new and challenging experience for Mickey, and he mustered all of his charm and charisma to meet it. After only a few dates, he began asking Ava to marry him. Her answer was short and simple: no. And she kept repeating it.

Back in North Carolina, Tommy Banks and his buddies wondered what had happened to the girl who pulled Tommy off his bike and gave him a kiss. She no longer waited for her ride home from Atlantic Christian College.

Then Tommy saw her picture in *The Wilson Daily Times*, Her name was Ava Gardner, he discovered, and she had gone to Hollywood!

"In 1941, I thought going to Hollywood was like going to Heaven," he recalled years later.

He cut out the article and put it in a shoe box—thus beginning a hobby that would mushroom beyond his wildest dreams.

In Durham, Duke University's Blue Devil football team was having a winning season that would lead to an invitation to the granddaddy of all bowl games—the Rose Bowl, to be played on New Year's Day in Pasadena, California.

Wade Talton, who got dropped by Ava after showing up late for a date because he'd been visiting another girl in Four Oaks, was a second-stringer on the Duke team.

He wrote to Ava and asked if she'd be willing to see him and some of his friends on the team while they were in California. She replied that she'd love to. She and Bappie would serve refreshments. "We'll have a good time," she wrote.

By then, it was widely known in North Carolina that Ava

had become a Hollywood "starlet."

"My stock went sky high with the other Duke players when they found out I had arranged for them to meet her," Wade recalled.

But on December 7, America awoke to the grim news that the Japanese had bombed the U.S. Naval base at Pearl Harbor, and the country was plunged into war.

Fearing an enemy attack on the West Coast, officials moved the Rose Bowl game to Duke. Despite Duke's twenty-to-sixteen victory over Oregon State, Wade's friends felt that they'd suffered a loss because they didn't get to go to California and meet Ava.

Wade and all the rest of Ava's friends back home were stunned at what they read in the newspaper only a couple of weeks after the relocated Rose Bowl game. On January 10, Ava had married Mickey Rooney in a small white church in Ballard, California. Ava wore a blue tailored suit. Only Bappie, Mickey's parents, and a handful of close Hollywood friends were present. The wedding was kept quiet until MGM chose to let the world know about it.

The headlines rivaled those accompanying the war news. An unknown MGM contract player from North Carolina, "the daughter of a poor sharecropper," according to the news stories, had married the biggest star in Hollywood.

Only five months earlier, on the eve of her departure for New York, Ava had sat on the front porch of the boarding house in Smithfield joking with her friends Alma Kilpatrick and Rudy Howell about how she was going to marry the biggest star in Hollywood. And now she had done just that. They could hardly believe it. Such things usually happened only in the movies.

Uncle Sam and Other Kin

Shortly after their marriage, Ava accompanied Mickey on a tour to boost War Bond sales. One of the scheduled stops was at Ft. Bragg near Fayetteville in eastern North Carolina, not far from where Ava had grown up.

The troops at Ft. Bragg were looking forward to seeing Ava more than Mickey. One of the soldiers, Sergeant Hubert Radford of Johnston County, had been assigned to present a huge bouquet of roses to her during Mickey's appearance. But Mickey accepted the flowers on his wife's behalf. She was at Inez's house in Raleigh, visiting family.

Mickey put on quite a performance for the troops at Ft. Bragg, but he put on a more impressive one in Raleigh, when he drove there after his appearance to meet his new kin for the first time.

Inez was in Rex Hospital, having given birth on January 24, to her third and last child, a son. Ava and Mickey caused quite a stir when they arrived to visit Inez and the new baby, John Michael Grimes, who would be called Michael. Mickey jokingly tried to talk Inez into calling her son Mickey. Michael, she told him, was close enough.

Ava's other sisters, except for Bappie, had come with their families to meet their new brother-in-law, and they cooked a big southern supper for him. Mickey showered attention on Mollie, keeping her laughing and giving her memories to treasure.

Many years later, Ava would say that she loved Mickey when she married him—and she loved him even when she ended their brief union. But she never loved him more than on that day in Raleigh when he made her mother so happy.

After the visit, Mickey and Ava went to Washington, where they and many other performers, including Jimmy Stewart, Betty Grable, and William Holden, celebrated President Franklin D. Roosevelt's birthday at the White House.

Ava wore a strapless black gown, and shortly after the big event her photo filled an entire page in a Washington newspaper. Only months earlier, Ava had been struggling to master typing and shorthand and wondering if she'd be able to find a secretarial job in Wilson and now she was at the White House with some of the most famous people on earth.

"It was unbelievable," she later would say.

Marrying Mickey Rooney brought Ava a generous dose of fame, and plenty of excitement, but it didn't do much for her career.

Her first appearances on screen went by so rapidly that folks back home had to keep their eyes open wide to spot her. She had bit parts in *Pilot No. 5* and *Hitler's Madman*. But regardless of how minuscule the role, if Ava's Rock Ridge School friends Alberta Cooney and Margie Williamson learned that she was going to be on screen, nothing could keep them away from the theater.

Alberta recalled that they went to see *Mighty Lak a Goat*, one of the many short "Our Gang" comedies that were shown prior to feature films. In it the character Buckwheat stirred up a chemical concoction that was meant to remove spots from clothes, but it ended up causing a horrible odor that clung to him, Spanky, and the other boys in the gang. They smelled mighty like a goat and were dismissed from school. The boys then went to a movie. The girl at the ticket window was Ava. All she was required to do was to look as though she smelled something awful.

When Ava raised her hand to fan away the odor, Alberta turned to Margie and said, "Look! She's wearing the watch Jack gave her for graduation!"

If Ava's career seemed to be going nowhere, her marriage was doing even worse.

Mickey, Ava later said, seemed to think that marriage

shouldn't change his life at all. He continued doing just as he had before marriage, including, Ava suspected, fooling around with other women. He denied it, but it didn't take Ava long to find proof. Only a year after their wedding, she left him.

She and Mickey Rooney were just children, and their lives were controlled by others, she later said. What chance did they ever really have?

Many years later, Mickey wrote in his autobiography what those who knew Ava in her early years didn't have to be told. She was an old-fashioned girl, he said, who was a virgin when he married her.

Mickey wasn't exactly an old-fashioned boy. Ava was the first of his eight wives.

Ava, left, and sister Bappie visiting at Inez's
in Raleigh at Christmas 1942.

One of Ava's countless "pin-up" photos
in her early years in Hollywood.

Sorrow and Success

Two headlines on the front page of *The Smithfield Herald* in May, 1943, told the story of the saddest day in Ava's life to that point.

"Ava Granted Divorce from Mickey Rooney," read one.

The article said that Mickey didn't show up for the court proceedings, and Ava testified that he told her repeatedly that their marriage was a mistake. She divorced him for mental cruelty and sought no alimony.

The other headline was cause for far greater grief: "Ava Gardner's Mother Dies in Raleigh."

Mollie Gardner died in Rex Hospital at 6:15 a.m. on May 21. She was fifty-nine.

Ava had seen her mother for the final time when she and Bappie came to Raleigh for a Christmas visit the previous December. Mollie was living with Inez and her family then.

Early in 1942, Mollie had begun bleeding abnormally, but ignored it. She didn't want to worry anyone, and didn't want to disrupt her work.

She continued her duties at the Rock Ridge Teacherage, and Emily Sheffield recalled that she would sometimes bend double in pain and take as many as ten aspirins at a time.

By the time Mollie went to a doctor, it was too late. Uterine cancer had spread throughout her body.

She remained at her job at the Teacherage until the end of the school year, then bade a tearful goodbye to the Sheffields and other teachers and friends and moved to Inez's house in Raleigh, where she was lovingly cared for during her remaining days.

The funeral was held at First Baptist Church in Smithfield on Sunday afternoon, May 23. The next issue of *The Herald* stated that burial was delayed until Monday, because Ava and Bappie were unable to make a flight connection from Los Angeles in time for the Sunday service. For Ava's and Bappie's benefit, a graveside service was conducted on Monday at Sunset Memorial Park, where Mollie was buried next to her beloved Jonas.

Ava and Bappie stayed for several days after the funeral to visit family and friends.

When Ava came to the Teacherage at Rock Ridge, Emily Sheffield later remembered, she stood gazing out her kitchen window and began to cry.

"It seems like I ought to be seeing Mama coming down those steps," she said.

Back in Hollywood, Ava dated an impressive list of famous men, including Howard Hughes, who was believed to be the richest man in America. He would pursue her for twenty years.

Ava's nephew Al Creech met Hughes during a two-week visit in 1943. Al was seventeen, and his parents had given him a trip to Hollywood as his high school graduation gift. The trains were jam-packed with servicemen, he later remembered, and he had to sit on his suitcase in the aisle for much of his trip.

When Ava's doorbell rang during his visit, Ava told Al, "If that's Howard Hughes, tell him I'm taking a bath. And offer him a drink." She went into a back room and closed the door.

Indeed, it was Howard Hughes, and Al offered him a drink. "He said he'd take a bourbon on the rocks, so I poured it for him and handed him the glass and a napkin," Al said.

By that time, Hughes had sat down by the telephone and was making one call after another. "He was the busiest man I'd ever seen," Al said. "He'd lift the glass as if he intended to take a swallow, but before he got it to his mouth he'd start talking again. I don't think he drank a single drop before he left."

Hughes threw a party at the famed nightclub Macombo during Al's visit but was too busy to attend. "He sent word to Ava to send him the bill," Al recalled, "and she did."

Al's date for the party was Ava's friend, starlet Peggy Malley. Al had his first experience with champagne that night, and later remembered laughingly that his legs felt "a little rubbery" when he got up from the table.

Howard Hughes had given Ava a German Shepherd named Hep whose special dinners were packed in cartons at a Los Angeles grocery store and neatly stacked in Ava's refrigerator.

Hep had a house in the back yard, but when it came time for a meal, he would carry his bowl to the back door and set it down. When he was let inside, he would open the refrigerator door and wait for someone to say, "Okay." Then he would take out one of his food cartons without disturbing the rest of the stack, close the refrigerator door, carry the carton outside, and place it in his bowl.

Only when somebody emptied the carton into his bowl and said, "Okay," would Hep begin eating.

"Of course if no one was there to open the carton, Hep could do it himself," Al said.

It was apparent to Al that Ava was not impressed with Howard Hughes' massive wealth. She complained that she couldn't walk down a street with him and have an ordinary conversation. If she noticed something in a store window and mentioned it was pretty, she said, it would be delivered to her door the next day.

During his stay in Hollywood, Al went bowling with Peggy Malley, Ava, and Mickey Rooney. "Ava and Mickey were just trying to be friends then," he said.

When it came time to return to North Carolina, Al learned that Hughes had arranged for him to have Pullman reservations. "I came home in style, and even got some money back for my train ticket," he remembered.

In July, 1944, Emily Sheffield, who was still at Rock Ridge, wrote to tell Ava that she was expecting another child. Ava wrote back the day she got the letter:

Dearest Emily,

I'm so ashamed of myself for not having written you before. I got a letter from Mr. Champion yesterday & I told Bappie then that I would probably get one from you & sure enough it arrived this morning.

I'm so thrilled about your little baby on the way. I do hope it's a girl. What does Dewey think about it or have you told him. I wonder if he'll be jealous since he's been your one and only for so long. Give him my love & a big hug & kiss for me.

I'm so happy you liked me in the picture (Three Men in White). Frankly, I thought it was a pretty bad picture but I did like my part. I had a fair part in the last Ann Southern picture called Masie Goes to Reno. It will be released in about two months & it really is a cute picture. I'm testing for the second lead in Lana Turner's next picture but I'm quite sure I won't get the part because if Susan Peters is well enough she is going to do it. But I'm happy that they even thought of me for the part.

How's everything around Rock Ridge? Give everybody my very best. Wish I could go home but the studio won't let me just now. I'm hoping to go next fall.

Thanks so much for the picture. It's so cute & I've got it up in my bedroom already. I'll send you one of my new ones as soon as I get them. They're pretty good. I wish you could pick out the one you like but I'll try to guess.

Write me again soon & give Mr. Sheffield my love.

Love & kisses
Ava

While Ava was playing small, but increasingly larger parts in movies, many of the people she knew were caught up in the war.

Her nephew Al joined the Army when he turned eighteen, not long after his visit with Ava, and was sent to Europe. His mother, Elsie Mae, went to the mailbox every day hoping for a letter from him. One day, she found a letter not from Al, but from Ava's former playmate and close friend, Shine.

He wrote that he had returned to his home as a young man. His father was married to a much younger woman, and he accused Shine of having an affair with her. His father tried to shoot him, he wrote, and the two wrestled with the gun. It went off, and his father fell dead.

Shine was in prison for life, and he asked Elsie Mae if she would send him a little money to buy cigarettes.

Whether Ava was ever told about Shine's sad fate isn't known.

Al still would be fighting in Europe when his father died from spinal meningitis at forty-two. Elsie Mae continued to run their store next to the Brogden Teacherage after her husband's death, as she would for more than twenty years.

Al wasn't the only one of Ava's relatives who went into the service during the war. Her brother Jack did, too, but was discharged early because of medical problems and spent the remainder of the war working in the shipyards at Newport News.

When he returned to Johnston County at war's end, Jack borrowed $5,000 from Ava and he and Al, who came home with three battle stars, started Gardner-Creech Oil Company in Smithfield. Jack later would also open a restaurant called the In and Out on Highway 301 between Smithfield and Selma.

Most of the boys Ava had known back at home got caught up in the war, too.

Bob Rose, with whom Ava had formed a couple one summer, had become an officer in the Marine Air Corps, and during a stopover in California he went to a USO dance in Hollywood. Lana Turner was there to entertain the troops and Bob ended up dancing with her. When he mentioned he had known Ava Gardner back at home, Lana went to a phone and called her. Soon afterward, Ava showed up, and she and Bob danced again as they had years earlier at Holt Lake.

Bob returned to Smithfield after his discharge and worked for Sanders General Store for a time before taking a job with the Ford agency at Cherry Point. He married, had two children, and later divorced.

Charles Barnes, who had lived across the road from the Rock Ridge Teacherage and had taken Ava to the June German, had ended up on a Navy attack transport in the Pacific during the war. "We had been scared to death, but were among the lucky ones who came home," he said. As his ship made its way back to California, Charles told some of his buddies that he knew Ava Gardner and would take them to Hollywood to meet her.

They didn't believe him but they went along with him to the USO in Los Angeles. Charles made a few calls and got Ava's number. She was surprised to hear his voice. He told her that he was at the USO with some of his buddies and they didn't believe that he knew her. "They've been trying to make me out to be a liar all the way across the Pacific," he recalled telling her.

"You wait right there," she said.

Not long afterward, Charles remembered, a limousine pulled up. Ava was driving.

She jumped out, threw her arms around him and gave him a kiss. Then she did the same for all of his buddies. "Their faces turned so red they looked like they were going to catch on fire," he said.

"Get in the wagon," Ava commanded. They all did, and she took them to her house.

"Do you boys want caviar or hot dogs?" she asked when they arrived. "Hot dogs are what you're gonna get," she added without waiting for an answer. Later, Charles and his buddies would think of those hot dogs as the most memorable they ever consumed.

"We sat on the veranda, and Ava talked about her days at Rock Ridge and wanted to know all the news I had from home," Charles recalled. "She talked about how much she missed her mother. And she asked my friends about their war experiences and all about their lives."

Charles returned to Rock Ridge and the family business, later married, raised a family, and went on to serve on the Wilson County Board of Commissioners.

Only later would Ava learn what had happened to some of her other friends during the war.

Mokie Stancil, who approved her dates at Holt Lake, served in the Army Air Corps. He married Betsy Atkinson of Raleigh, a former May Queen at Woman's College in Greensboro, in 1946.

They would rear three children as Mokie built a successful oil dealership in Selma. He became one of Johnston County's most prominent civic leaders.

Wade Talton was an officer in the Navy. He returned home and joined his brother Hubie in the family's furniture, appliance, and grocery businesses in Smithfield. Wade married Vera Lanning of Walburg, N.C., and they had a daughter. Hubie Talton married Catherine Stewart, who lived near Four Oaks, and they had a son. Hubie was a member of the Smithfield Board of Commissioners for ten years, and he later served as mayor and town manager.

St. Clair Pugh, also an officer in the Navy, went to New York after the war and became a copy editor for Doubleday. He went on to a lengthy career with the *New York Daily News*, *New York Post*, and *New York Newsday*.

Bubsy Sugg, whose blue eyes made such an impression on Ava, served in the Army, then began a career with the U.S. Postal Service in Smithfield. He married Hallie Mae Daughtry of Selma, and they had two daughters.

Ava's cousin Fred Gardner married his high school sweetheart, Ava's friend Alma Kilpatrick, with whom she had spent the night before going to New York for her screen test, and they had four children. Fred worked as a parole officer and later as a retirement counselor with the state treasurer's office. He and Alma were killed in a car wreck in 1979.

The end of the war changed Ava's life, too, because band leader Artie Shaw also returned from the service. A mutual friend introduced the two at a party, and Ava couldn't believe she was actually meeting the man to whose music she had danced at Holt Lake. She was immediately smitten.

Artie was much more than a band leader. He was considered to be a genius as composer and performer, believed by some to be the greatest clarinetist ever. His 1938 recording of Cole Porter's "Begin the Beguine" made him famous and had been proclaimed a classic. But it was more than talent, charm and good looks that impressed Ava about Artie. She later said that he was the first true intellectual she'd ever encountered.

Ava and Artie began going out every night, and on October

17, 1945, they were married at Artie's Beverly Hills mansion. Ava wore a blue tailored suit similar to the one she wore to marry Mickey Rooney.

As soon as they were married Artie began pressuring her to do something about her lack of education, Ava recalled, and she enrolled in extension courses at UCLA to appease him.

Until she married Artie, the only book Ava had read to completion was *Gone With The Wind*. Now Artie assigned her reading lists, and she plowed through Dostoyevsky's *The Brothers Karamazov*, Thomas Mann's *Magic Mountain* and other serious works.

One day Artie came home and found Ava reading the steamy new novel *Forever Amber*. He snatched it from her, threw it across the room and scolded her for reading such trash.

Ava would come to deeply resent the way Artie frequently belittled her for her intellectual and educational shortcomings, sometimes in front of others.

For Ava, good things often were accompanied by bad, and that would prove to be the case in 1946. MGM loaned her out for two movies that year: Allied Artists' *Whistle Stop*, with George Raft; and Universal Studio's *The Killers*, with a handsome twenty-two-year-old newcomer who had been a circus acrobat, Burt Lancaster.

The Killers was based on an Ernest Hemingway short story. Later, Ava would do two more films taken from Hemingway's work, *The Snows of Kilimanjaro*, and *The Sun Also Rises*, and Hemingway would say that she was the only actor who portrayed his characters the way he envisioned them. Eventually they would become close friends.

After the film was finished, Ava and her young co-star posed for publicity pictures doing acrobatics on the beach, and Ava got the chance to demonstrate the handstands and other tricks she'd learned as a girl in Brogden. (Years later, Ava would be photographed teaching famed film costume designer Edith Head how to stand on her head.)

Ava got fine reviews from *The Killers*, a film that later would be credited with launching both her and her Burt Lancaster to stardom.

• • •

But only a year after their wedding, Artie Shaw stunned Ava by asking for a divorce. Later, she would credit Artie with stirring in her a lifelong interest in art, literature, classical music, religion, philosophy and politics. And she would take great delight in noting that for his next wife, the fourth of the eight he eventually would have, he chose Kathleen Winsor, author of *Forever Amber*.

Artie never came to North Carolina to meet the Gardner family, but he did leave a tribute to Ava's roots—a musical composition found many years later in her extensive record collection. It was a swing tune titled "The Grabtown Grapple," which Artie co-wrote and recorded in 1946.

The success of *The Killers* prompted MGM to cast Ava in *The Hucksters* with Clark Gable and newcomer Deborah Kerr in 1947. Not only was her childhood dream of being a movie star coming true, but she was going to be in a movie with her mother's favorite actor.

Oh, how she wished, she told family and friends, that her mother could have lived to see it.

Ava's role in *The Killers*, (1946) boosted her to stardom.

Becoming a Star

In 1949, Ava joined a big-name cast to make *The Great Sinner*, which was loosely based on Dostoyevsky's *The Gambler*. It starred Gregory Peck. This would be the first of three films that Ava and Greg, as she always called him, would make together (the other two would be *The Snows of Kilimanjaro* and *On the Beach*), and while they were making it, they would become close, lifelong friends.

Despite Ava's protestations that she was no actress, Peck ranked her among the better screen actresses and thought she had the potential for greatness. He became her coach and adviser as well as friend.

When *The Great Sinner* came out later that year, a premiere was held at the Howell Theater in Smithfield. And although neither Ava nor any of the other stars (Melvyn Douglas, Walter Huston, Ethel Barrymore and Agnes Moorehead also appeared in it) attended, it stirred great excitement in Johnston County. Ava mailed autographed tickets to all of her family and friends.

Ava had come home earlier that year for a big bash thrown in her honor by the Smithfield Chamber of Commerce. A dance was held at the Country Club of Johnston County, near Holt Lake, and Ava was presented the key to the city by Dr. William Massey, a dentist who was Smithfield's mayor.

Vivia Rives Creech of Smithfield recalled that Ava wore a simple and elegant royal blue satin cocktail suit that night, and "was the most beautiful thing we'd ever seen."

The men who danced with her weren't able to make more than a step or two before another cut in. Their wives and girlfriends looked on in awe. "We were all star-struck that night," Vivia said.

Full stardom came to Ava in 1951 with her appearance as the tragic and beautiful Julie Laverne in the musical *Show Boat*. Judy Garland, Lena Horne, and Dinah Shore had been considered for the role, but it went to Ava, who thought that her friend Lena should have gotten it (Ava always maintained that Lena, Katharine Hepburn and Greta Garbo were the three most beautiful women in the world, although it would be Ava that the press soon would label "The World's Most Beautiful Woman.")

Show Boat would become the biggest grossing film of 1951, and Ava would be widely hailed for her performance.

Remarkably, *Show Boat* had other North Carolina connections besides Ava. It was based on a 1926 novel by Edna Ferber. Although the story was set on the Mississippi River, Ferber had built it around an actual show boat that went from town to town along the North Carolina coast, and she had lived in the historic town of Bath while she was researching it.

One of Ava's co-stars in the film was the magnificent soprano Kathryn Grayson, who spent the first two years of her life in Winston-Salem.

During the filming, the dance Ava and Kathryn's characters did on deck was dubbed "The Carolina Shuffle" by the cast and crew. And Robert Sterling, who played the husband of Ava's character, was the real-life husband of actress Anne Jeffreys, a native of Goldsboro.

Ava had one crushing disappointment about *Show Boat*. She had sung in *The Killers*, and had rehearsed hard for her part as Julie Laverne. But at the last minute the studio decided to dub Annette Warren's voice for hers. Ava's voice was used on the *Show Boat* sound track album, however.

Proof of Ava's stardom came when *Time* magazine featured her on its cover after the success of *Show Boat*. (She remains one of only four North Carolina natives to share that distinction. The others: Billy Graham, Senator Sam Ervin, and Senator Jesse Helms.)

Over the next two decades, the peak years of her career, Ava's image would grace more than 3,000 magazine covers worldwide.

Soon after Ava's success in Show Boat, part of Ava's past came to Hollywood. A movie called *Carbine*, about the life of David Marshall "Carbine" Williams, who invented the carbine rifle while in prison, was filmed by MGM, starring Jimmy Stewart as Carbine.

Carbine and his wife, Maggie, who had been Ava's first grade teacher, came to Hollywood to watch the filming. Ava and Bappie went to the set to see the Williamses and recall old times. Carbine had become wildly flamboyant with his new wealth, and during the visit, he took Ava's hand, placed something on her palm, and closed her fingers around it.

Ava opened her hand to find a small velvet pouch with several large diamonds inside.

"Of course Ava couldn't accept such a gift," Bappie recalled. "But she did appreciate Carbine's generosity."

Some people who knew Ava before she went to Hollywood thought that stardom might change her, but they soon discovered that it didn't. She was still the same down-to-earth Ava she always had been, still kept her close ties to home, still loved the people, places and things she always had loved, including North Carolina country cooking.

Johnny Grant, a native of Goldsboro, a top Los Angeles radio personality, was Honorary Mayor of Hollywood and emcee for many of Bob Hope's tours to entertain American troops. He remembered that every time he came home to visit kin, he took barbecue back for Ava.

Whenever family went to see Ava, they carried along sacks of Atkinson's corn meal, jars of homemade peach brandy and other of Ava's favorite comestibles. Her great niece Ava Carol Creech would remember holding a homemade coconut cake in her lap throughout one entire flight.

93

• • •

Friends and family never knew when Ava might just pop in. Marilyn Coltrane, who had been Mokie Stancil's girlfriend during Ava's days at Holt Lake, married Ben Gammons, had two sons, and moved to Massachusetts. Marilyn's sister, Doris, was married to Joe Grimes, brother of Ava's brother-in-law Johnnie Grimes.

Marilyn had lived with her grandmother, Mrs. T.R. Hood, during high school and college and while her husband was in the Army. Her grandmother was now bedridden at her home on South Second Street in Smithfield, and Marilyn was visiting her one day after Ava had become a star. She had been thinking about Ava, she said, and was dusting furniture in her grandmother's living room when the doorbell rang.

"When I opened the door, I heard a husky voice say, 'Hello, Marilyn,' and there stood the most beautiful Ava Gardner in a full-length sable coat."

Marilyn was almost immobilized. She dropped her dust cloth. "I stuttered 'A-Ava!'" she said.

Ava had heard that Marilyn's grandmother was in declining health, and wanted to see her. "I was so excited I don't remember how I showed her down the hall to Granny's bedroom," Marilyn said. "She went right over to Granny's bed and was just as sweet as she could be. I left her alone with her while I went to get my husband to come meet her. She spent some quality time with Granny, and they really hit it off."

Ava's stardom brought occasional small benefits to

Ava's sister, Myra Pearce, appeared on "I've Got a Secret," with Garry Moore, in the early 1950s. Photos made by nephew Billy Grimes.

some family members. Her sister Myra got a free trip to New York to appear on the popular network television show, "I've Got a Secret," hosted by Garry Moore. A brunette beauty who looked a lot like her younger sister, Myra didn't long keep her secret that she was Ava Gardner's sister.

Ava's wardrobe grew so big that she often sent clothing to family members who might be able to wear it. One beneficiary was her niece, Mary Edna Grimes, daughter of Inez and Johnnie, who by this time had moved to Smithfield, where Johnnie operated his own auto parts business. Mary Edna, a student at Smithfield High School, shared her aunt's striking beauty, although she was shorter. A few alterations were required, but she could wear a lot of the clothes Ava sent.

Some she just didn't like, though, and these usually ended up at the Salvation Army. One such was a suit with a dark jacket accented with abstract white flowers that Ava had worn on a date with Howard Hughes.

Hughes hated being photographed, and because of his reclusive nature and wariness it rarely happened. But one photographer managed to snap a shot of him and Ava on that date. It would be published countless times around the world in years to come.

Somewhere in North Carolina someone surely ended up wearing that famous suit without a clue about its history or what it might eventually have been worth.

Some things about Ava's stardom didn't set well with her family.

When Ava used the term "dirt poor" to describe her early years, the studio publicity mill made a big thing of it, and it would follow her the rest of her life. To Ava, that just meant the hard times that she and everybody she knew had lived through during the Depression. But the image that many took from it was that Ava and her family lacked sufficient food, clothing and shelter—the kind of poverty that was never experienced by the Gardners. And some in the family resented that.

A similar thing happened when Ava talked of going barefoot

Ava became a blonde briefly in the early 1950s.

as a girl. The impression many got was that her family was too poor to buy shoes. But the reality was that it was something she loved doing.

When Ava referred to herself as a "little hillbilly," she meant she was a country girl—but many came to think she had grown up in the mountains of North Carolina, which were hundreds of miles from her childhood home.

Even Ava's name came to cause confusion, and resentment to her family. Shortly after she arrived in Hollywood, a studio publicist decided that Ava Gardner sounded too glamorous for a dirt-poor country girl, and out went a news release stating that her real name was Lucy Johnson, and it had been changed by the studio, just as Marion Morrison's name had been changed to John Wayne and Doris von Kapplehoff's to Doris Day.

Lucy Johnson would continue to be listed as the real name of Ava Gardner in trivia books and other publications throughout the years. During the TV quiz show "Jeopardy" in the 1980s, the contestants were stumped by: "When she was growing up in North Carolina, she was known as Lucy Johnson." North Carolina fourth graders were given the same misinformation about Ava in their social studies textbook through the 1990s.

Nothing bothered Ava's family more than the scandal mongering publications such as *Confidential* magazine and the supermarket tabloids that fabricated so many lurid stories about Ava and her escapades over several decades.

That all began when she started seeing Frank Sinatra.

The Sinatra They All Loved

Ava met Frank Sinatra while she was married to Mickey Rooney. He was a huge star at the time.

A native of Hoboken, New Jersey, he had been a vocalist with the Tommy Dorsey band in the late 1930s, and had become the first teen idol. Hordes of young girls, called "bobby-soxers," screamed, wept and swooned at the sight of his almost painfully thin, boyish body, and his dreamy eyes were every bit as blue, Ava couldn't help but notice, as Bubsy Sugg's back in Johnston County.

Ava had heard a lot of gossip about Frank and his fondness for beautiful women, and he flirted with her on their first meeting. But she knew he was Catholic, married and had children, and she didn't go out with married men. Over the coming years, she encountered him occasionally, and they became friends, but just that. Everything changed, though, when he showed up at a party where she and Bappie were houseguests in Palm Springs in 1949.

Ava would remember that as the night she fell in love with the man who would be the love of her life. By that time, Frank's career had hit a low ebb, and his marriage was coming to an end. But it would take two years before he finally was divorced. Before that happened, the press would discover their affair, and Ava would be painted as the scarlet woman who broke up Frank's happy home.

Ava and Frank were quietly married on November 7, 1951, at the home of Lester Sachs, a cousin of Frank's manager, in Philadelphia. They moved into the Hampshire House in New York. Ava's Rock Ridge School friend Alberta, who was married to Bill Luehrs and living in Washington, read about it in the newspaper, and decided to give Ava a call.

It had been several years since they had been in touch, but Alberta had no hesitancy about being straight-forward and joking with Ava.

"Why did you marry that skinny thing?" she asked. "Do you really love him?"

"Oh, Alberta—yes, yes," she recalled Ava saying. "I really do love him."

Late in the summer of 1952, Ava's nephew Billy Grimes, son of her sister Inez, and three of his friends from Smithfield took a trip to New York before plunging back into their studies at the University of North Carolina.

Billy's friends were Robert Farmer, who eventually became a superior court judge; Albert Farmer Jr., who became a physician specializing in endocrinology; and Austin Stevens, who became a district court judge.

Billy, who became a Smithfield businessman, liked classical music, and one of his main purposes in going to New York was to attend the Metropolitan Opera. His friends just wanted to see the Yankees play.

Billy also wanted to see his aunt, and he called when they got to New York. Ava told him that Frank had reserved a table that night for Billy and his friends at Bill Miller's Riviera Supper Club in Fort Lee, N.J., where Frank was appearing.

Frank's television show had been canceled and his contract with Capital Records was not being renewed. He was fearful of becoming a has-been, but that night he put on a performance that Ava's nephew and his buddies would never forget.

One of the songs he sang was "My Boy Bill," from the musical *Carousel*, which he dedicated to Billy.

Billy stayed in New York a few days longer than planned, and he went with Ava and Frank to the premiere of *The Snows of Kilimanjaro* at the huge Rivoli Theatre.

He had brought a suit with him, but Ava said it wouldn't do. He had to have a tuxedo. At the last minute Frank sent him to a nearby theatrical costume shop where he was properly outfitted.

•   •   •

When a limousine arrived to take Ava, Frank, and Billy to the Rivoli, Billy got in last. As they neared the theater, Billy couldn't believe what he was seeing. "There were twenty thousand people there," he said. "Police barricades were up, and spotlights and flash-bulbs were everywhere. There were at least fifty Pinkerton guards trying to control the crowd."

A uniformed attendant stepped to the limousine and opened the door where Billy sat.

"Okay, Billy, here's your big moment," Frank told him.

Billy crawled out to face the crowd and heard a voice shout, "Hey Billy! Where'd you get the suit?"

Earl Wilson had included an item in his popular column about Frank sending Billy to a costume shop to rent his tux.

"There I was in all my splendor, and I was embarrassed," Billy recalled with a laugh.

The next day, Ava was scheduled to return to the Rivoli to autograph photos in the lobby.

"The lobby looked as big as a football field," Billy remembered. "People were coming in off the street in droves, and when the movie ended and thousands more poured into the lobby, things really got hairy."

Someone quickly whisked Ava away, and Billy stood won-

dering what to do. Then a burly man with a gun under his coat grabbed him and rushed him into an alley to a waiting car. The man was Hank Sanicola, Frank's bodyguard. "He really saved my bacon that day," Billy said.

One evening, Billy accompanied Ava and Frank to Club 21 for a party hosted by someone whose name he has long since forgotten. He did recall that he was seated next to the host, and he got a clear look at the tab for the evening—$15,000 for about twenty people.

Ava, her mother, Mollie, and nephew Billy Grimes at Rock Ridge.

99

Billy also attended a Giants-Dodgers baseball game at the Polo Grounds with Ava and Frank. They were the only three in the twenty-seat box owned by famed restaurateur Toots Shore. "It must not have been an important game that day," Billy said.

Frank and Ava left Billy at the Hampshire House one day while they went to an engagement. Billy didn't mind. He wanted to watch TV. Back home, TV was a single perpetually snowy channel. But New York had several clear channels. Unfortunately, the TV in the Sinatra quarters wasn't functioning. Frank's manager, Manie Sachs, also lived in the Hampshire House, and since he was not going to be home that day, Frank told Billy to watch TV at Manie's place.

Another client of Manie's was singer Mario Lanza, who Frank called "the fat Italian." Mario had a powerful operatic voice and hits on the pop music charts. One of his best-loved songs was "Be My Love."

When the phone rang in Manie's apartment, Billy wasn't sure whether to answer or not, but he did—and on the other end of the line was Mario Lanza.

Billy jotted down a message for Manie, and when he saw Frank and Ava later that day he couldn't conceal his excitement at having actually spoken to Mario Lanza. "I have every one of his records!" he exclaimed, a *faux pas* he recognized immediately.

On their first meeting, Frank had asked Billy what he was majoring in at UNC.

"Journalism," Billy told him.

"Oh Jesus, not that!" Frank said.

Now, having heard how many Mario Lanza records he had, Frank asked how many Sinatra records Billy owned.

Billy sheepishly replied, "Uh...uh...." And finally acknowledged that he didn't yet have any.

Frank threw up his hands. "See?" he said to Ava. "I get no respect."

Billy felt awful about his slip-up, and the next day he went out and bought the first of what he announced would be his Sinatra collection. Frank autographed the album, "To my boy Bill. Have fun!—Frankie."

On the same day that Billy had a ticket to the Metropolitan Opera, Frank was scheduled to have his final recording session at

Capitol Records. Frank told Billy how to get to the Capitol Records building and invited him to sit in on his session after the opera.

Billy saw Puccini's *La Boheme*, a tragic love story in which the heroine dies of pneumonia. And he reached Capitol Records in time to hear fifteen minutes or so of Frank's final session. He was singing "Why Try to Change Me Now?"

When Frank and Billy returned to the Hampshire House, Ava met them at the door.

"Well! What whorehouse have you two been to?" she exclaimed.

"Whorehouse?" Billy replied. "I've been to an opera house!"

"That's the worst excuse I've ever heard!" Ava responded.

As Billy was leaving to return home, Frank followed him out of the Hampshire House and asked if he had cab fare. Billy told him he was in good shape financially. He still had forty dollars in his pocket, more than enough to get him home.

But Frank—who was nearly broke and unsure of his future—insisted on giving Billy a hundred-dollar bill. He wouldn't take no for an answer, Billy remembered.

In September of 1952, several weeks after Billy's visit, Ava brought Frank home to meet the rest of the Gardner clan. They gathered at Myra's home in Winston-Salem. Myra and her husband, Bronnie Pearce, had opened a successful laundry in Winston-Salem, with pick-up-and-delivery diaper service, and had a daughter, Myra Jean, and two sons, Bronnie Clifton and Melvin Gardner.

Ava's niece, Mary Edna Grimes, Billy's sister, then a high school senior, recalled that Frank was very nice, and seemed a bit shy. Her brother, Michael, who was born when Ava came home with Mickey Rooney, was ten now. He remembered that he and Frank were alone for a time in the living room. Frank sat on the piano stool, Michael on the floor in front of him, and they talked about Michael's new venture at school, where he was learning to play the clarinet, the instrument that had brought fame and fortune to Artie Shaw.

If the discussion raised jealous thoughts in Frank, he kept them hidden. He told Michael about learning to play the flute when he was a boy.

Bronnie celebrated his birthday during Frank's visit. When the cake and refreshments were served, Frank joined in singing "Happy Birthday." What a serenade his uncle was receiving, Billy recalled thinking.

Several maids scurried about the Pearce residence during the weekend, cleaning and taking care of laundry for guests. Not until Al Creech got home to Smithfield and unpacked his suitcase did he realize there'd been a mixup in the laundry. He had a pair of Frank's underwear—silk Jockey shorts in a very small size. Later, he wouldn't recall what became of this dubious keepsake.

While still in Winston-Salem, Frank and Ava appeared at a Democratic rally in support of presidential candidate Adlai Stevenson, who was waging an uphill battle against Dwight D. Eisenhower. It would be their last appearance together in North Carolina.

In 1952, Ava went to Africa to film Mogambo, with Clark Gable and Grace Kelly, who would become a lifelong friend.

Remarkably, *Mogambo* was a remake of *Red Dust*, the movie Ava saw with her mother at the Howell Theater when she was nine.

Gable was again the big game hunter, and Ava played Honey-Bear Kelly, the role she had watched Jean Harlow portray twenty years earlier.

Frank's career was still going nowhere, and pressures from that were causing stress between him and Ava. Their fights were frequent and melodramatic to the point of Frank feigning suicide by firing a bullet into a mattress.

Plans were in the works to film *From Here to Eternity,* James Jones' Pulitzer-Prize-winning novel about Army life in Hawaii prior to the attack on Pearl Harbor. Frank had read the book and felt that he had been born to play the part of the scrappy little Italian, Private Angelo Maggio.

No one thought of him for the role, however, and no one would listen to his pleas for an audition. Ava wielded her influence to get him the audition, and she wasn't surprised that he won the role.

When Academy Awards night rolled around in 1953, Ava

and Frank were present. She was nominated as Best Actress for *Mogambo*, and Frank was up for Best Supporting Actor.

Several critics were confident that Ava would win, but the Oscar went instead to newcomer Audrey Hepburn for *Roman Holiday*.

The award for Best Picture went to *From Here to Eternity*. And Frank won, too, sending his career soaring again.

Jealousy, alcohol, and the separations and demands brought by their thriving careers gradually tore Frank's and Ava's marriage asunder, and they divorced in 1957. Although they couldn't live together, Ava said that she would love Frank for as long as she lived. And she had no doubt that he felt the same about her.

After their divorce, Bappie remembered, Frank sent Ava a huge bouquet on her birthday every year. After the flowers faded and died, Ava left them in their special place on her dresser until a fresh bouquet arrived on the following Christmas Eve.

Billy Grimes, left, with his Aunt Ava and her husband, Frank Sinatra, during break in Sinatra's performance at the Riviera Supper Club in New Jersey in the summer of 1952.

Leaving America

The Barefoot Contessa would end up being the movie that most people identified with Ava. She made it in Rome in 1954.

It opened with a graveside scene and mourners standing under dark umbrellas. It was about a beautiful Spanish woman who had been born in poverty, achieved fame and fortune as an actress, but never found fulfillment in her personal life.

Many moviegoers thought the plot closely resembled Ava's own life. But Ava felt it was like Rita Hayworth's.

During the filming of *The Barefoot Contessa*, Ava had problems with both her director, Joe Mankiewicz, and her co-star, Humphrey Bogart, who needled her constantly, calling her the Grabtown Gypsy. She also had more unpleasant encounters with the press, which falsely reported that she had arrived at her hotel drunk, disorderly and barefoot (that part was true), and went on a rampage.

Despite her problems, the movie gave Ava some of her most cherished scenes and introduced her to flamenco dancing, which became one of the great joys of her life.

Ava had begun an affair with Spain's most famous bullfighter, Luis Miguel Dominguin, after her breakup with Frank and she went to Madrid to see him after filming *The Barefoot Contessa*. While there, she ended up in a hospital with kidney stones, and Luis Miguel brought Ernest Hemingway to the hospital to meet her, the beginning of their friendship.

Back at home, as a favor to her friend Sammy Davis Jr., one of Frank Sinatra's closest pals, Ava agreed to pose for a cover for *Ebony* magazine. Somebody sold photos taken of her and Sammy during that shoot to *Confidential* magazine, which used them to create a false scandal, that Ava and Sammy were having an affair.

Ava also had another unpleasant encounter with Howard Hughes who was trying to convince her to marry him, resulting in the end of her romance with Luis Miguel.

Her life was in something of a mess. She hated Hollywood, hated the press, hated the attention she constantly drew, and she began thinking of moving to Spain.

She had first fallen on love with that country in 1950 when she filmed *Pandora and the Flying Dutchman* in the ancient village of Tossa de Mar on the Mediterranean coast with James Mason. She liked the countryside, the villages, the simple way of life she found there.

She bought a house outside Madrid and moved there in December, 1955, shortly before she turned thirty-three. Her friend Reenie Jordan, whose formal name was Mearene, went with her. Ava had hired Reenie as a housekeeper in 1947 and they had found that they had similar outlooks on life and similar senses of humor—Reenie always said that Ava should have been a comedienne. They became best friends, and Reenie began filling a role in Ava's life that was much like Bappie's. One or both were always with Ava to see her through the fiercest storms of life, although Reenie and Bappie still retained their own homes in California. Actually, Reenie, who was black, got along better with Ava than Bappie because Ava and Bappie were opposites in many ways and started getting on one another's nerves if they stayed together very long. Also Reenie was closer in age to Ava.

Reenie remained until Ava was settled in Spain, then returned home. But she always rushed to Ava's side whenever she called.

In Spain, Ava later said, she felt at home for the first time since she left North Carolina in the summer of 1941. Although she would return home for visits, she would never again live in the United States.

Later, Ava sold the house and moved into a large apartment building in Madrid to be closer to the nightlife. She loved giving parties and often hired gypsy musicians to play so she and her guests could dance the flamenco long into the night.

Her neighbor in the adjoining apartment was Juan Peron, the deposed dictator of Argentina. Peron once called the police to complain about the noise from Ava's apartment. Vibration from all the flamenco dancing, he claimed, had caused an urn to topple off a shelf in his apartment. It was later reported that the urn contained the ashes of Peron's wife, Eva, a one-time actress whose life would later be portrayed in the musical and film *Evita*.

Ava made two trips home to visit family with Walter Chiari, an Italian actor with whom she began a relationship after appearing with him in *The Little Hut* in 1957.

Tom Capps, who had rescued Ava from the Brogden School water tower, was sound asleep with his wife Minnie one winter night in their home not far from the house where they lived when Ava was born in Grabtown.

At about two in the morning, their daughter Ruby, who was older than Ava, was awakened by the sound of ice crunching on the dirt road in front of their house. She heard car doors open and shut and footsteps coming toward the house, then a knock. Ruby went to the door to find Ava and Walter Chiari. Ava wanted to surprise Tom and Minnie and went to the bedroom and awakened them herself. The elderly couple sat on the bed and talked until Ava and Walter decided to go.

On Ava's next trip home with Walter, they had a stormy falling out at her brother's house in Smithfield. Ava told Jack to send him packing.

Jack was more than happy to drive his Italian guest to the Raleigh-Durham Airport. He bade him goodbye and good luck, then drove home to Smithfield with thoughts of a peaceful evening ahead. He walked into his living room, dusted off his hands and said, "Well, that's that."

His proclamation was met by an odd silence. Then he turned and saw why. On his couch sat Walter Chiari, who had taken a taxi from the airport and beaten Jack back to his house by several minutes.

Ava's great niece, Ava Carol Creech, daughter of Al and his

At the Stork Club in New York in 1962, Ava's niece, Ava Carol Creech, received a rose from Italian film star Walter Chiari.

former wife, Verlia, got to visit Ava and Walter in New York when she was twelve. Ava Carol and her younger brother, David, had spent many happy times with Ava in North Carolina, Hollywood and New York.

When they were small, Ava Carol remembered, Ava would cuddle them close, smell their hair and say, "Oh you smell so good!"

Among the many places Ava and Walter took Ava Carol during her trip to New York was the Stork Club. While they were there, a photographer captured Walter presenting Ava Carol a long-stemmed rose while a beaming Ava looked on, the affection for her namesake clear in her expression.

As a teenager, Ava Carol and Ava would see Barbra Streisand in *Funny Girl* on Broadway. The next day, Barbra and her then husband Elliott Gould entertained them in their Park Avenue apartment.

"They spent most of the afternoon showing card tricks," Ava Carol recalled.

Ava Carol's favorite times were those she spent alone with Ava. "I got to know her as a woman, not just a relative or an actress on a movie screen," she said. "I learned that she was very human."

She recalled Ava showing her a script of *On the Beach*, which she filmed with Gregory Peck in Australia in 1959. It was about nuclear holocaust.

On the script margins, Ava had made notations to help her bring emotions to the screen based on her own experiences.

Later, Bappie said that that movie had a lasting impact on Ava, and she re-read the script many times long after the film was released.

In November, 1960, St. Clair Pugh, Ava's friend from Holt Lake days, partied with her during her stay in the Regency Hotel in New York. It was the first time he had seen her since she went to Hollywood.

They sat up late talking. "She told me I was just a little boy when I took her to the mid-winter dances at Chapel Hill," St. Clair recalled.

At three in the morning, Ava remembered that her niece, Mary Edna, had just had a baby boy, and she decided to call right then and congratulate her.

Mary Edna's husband, Norman Grantham, called Brick, a dentist, was a lieutenant in the Air Force stationed at Craig Air Force Base at Selma, Alabama. And Mary Edna and her baby, who

was named for his father, were in the base hospital. Ava soon learned that not even movie stars could break through military rules.

No congratulatory calls went into Air Force hospital maternity wards at three in the morning, St. Clair remembered, no matter who was making them.

Ava and niece, Mary Edna Grantham, (standing at higher level) during a family visit in 1959.

• • •

Brick Grantham was promoted to captain and stationed in Evreau, France, when the couple's second child, a daughter, Mary Linda, was born in the base hospital in March, 1962. They later would have another daughter, Elizabeth Rose, born in Smithfield.

During their time in France, Mary Edna and her husband went to Madrid twice, once to visit Ava and again to stay in her apartment while she was away.

They were accompanied on their first visit by Brick's sister, Cinda, and his first cousin, Lena Rose Patterson, who were college students at the time and soon would continue their sightseeing tour of Europe.

Ava was filming *55 Days at Peking* with Charlton Heston then, and Mary Edna and Brick got to see how hard she worked. There was no partying. Ava worked on her lines at night and was up at dawn to get to the set.

Mary Edna and Brick visited the set twice. Ava introduced them to Charlton Heston, his wife and daughter, and others in the cast and crew. Mary Edna went into Ava's dressing room, where she was preparing to have photos made to publicize the film.

"She had on a beautiful gown," Mary Edna said. "She was into chess at that time (Artie Shaw had taught her how to play), and she had a chess board set up in a corner of the dressing room. She also had music playing that would help her stay in the mood of her character."

The movie was about westerners caught up in the Boxer Rebellion in 1900. It was being filmed on the largest set ever constructed for a single production.

A replica of Peking had been built on a seventy-acre barley field fifteen miles outside Madrid—and it was surrounded by a canal and a forty-foot-high wall. More than 6,500 Chinese residents of England and France had been hired as extras to populate the city, which could be viewed in full only from the air and would be blown up for the film's finale.

Ava had become enamored by Spain's most famous sport, and during a break in filming, she took Mary Edna and Brick to a bullfight and explained all the intricacies of it. That night, Ava took them on a tour of the small food specialty shops in Madrid, and they ended up at a popular local nightspot.

"Ava got up and danced the flamenco that night," Mary Edna recalled. "Many of the people in the club looked like gypsies."

Another night, Ava took them to fine nightclub for dinner at eleven. By the time of their departure, Mary Edna and Brick were glad Ava had been tied up with her movie during most of their visit. "We were worn out," Mary Edna said.

At 36, Ava appeared in *The Naked Maja* (1959) and was still considered to be one of the most beautiful women in the world.

Incognito

During her visits home, Ava usually stayed with Inez and Johnnie Grimes in Smithfield, and she would arrive with nearly enough luggage to fill the house.

Johnnie would greet her with mock dread and ask, "How long are you planning on staying this time?"

"Not long enough to wear out my welcome," Ava always replied.

She adored Johnnie and enjoyed their little ritual at the beginning of each visit. She was also close to Johnnie's brothers, Joe and Ben, and their families in Smithfield. She often summoned Joe to Johnnie's house to play bridge into the wee hours.

When she arrived at the Raleigh-Durham Airport, Ava usually would be wearing a nondescript T-shirt, jeans, and a pair of cheap "flip-flops." Her hair would be covered with a scarf, and there were the usual sunglasses for incognito travel. She was rarely recognized.

In Hollywood, Ava's favorite hairdresser had been the famed Sydney Guilaroff, an artist who made a fortune by turning his talent from brushes and paints to combs and curlers. But whenever Ava came to Smithfield, her favorite hairdresser was Ruby Daughtry, who operated Ruby's Beauty Salon in her home on South Third Street. Her advertising slogan was "I Need Your Head In My Business."

Ruby would arrange for Ava to come when she had no other customers.

"Ava's beautiful hair was shoulder-length," Ruby said. "Her lips were just as pink as they could be, and she didn't need a bit of makeup. She didn't care what she looked like. All she wanted was clean hair, and a day after she'd been to see me she'd put that hair up under a toboggan and take her dog for a walk. And nobody would recognize her."

After the death of her husband, Leamon Daughtry, Ruby married Ralph Davis, who had worn Ava's tennis shoes during their school days at Brogden.

Ralph had a successful plumbing, heating, and air-conditioning business in Smithfield. One day he and his helpers were working outdoors on a plumbing job when Ava came down the street with her dog on a leash and a toboggan on her head.

When she saw Ralph, she rushed over and gave her old friend a kiss on the cheek.

"Ralph, who was that woman?" one of his helpers asked, after Ava had walked on.

"Oh, that was Ava Gardner," Ralph said.

"Yeah, sure," his helpers replied.

"She was a wonderful person," Ruby said. "She'd often invite me and Ralph to come over to Jack's, and we'd sit around and talk and just have a great time."

As years went by, Ava wanted less and less hoopla and no movie star treatment, which her brother Jack couldn't always understand.

Once, Jack wanted to host a party for Ava at a country club in Raleigh, but she would have none of it.

Ava's brother, Jack, served several terms in the North Carolina legislature in the 1970s.

At that time, her niece, Mary Edna, and her husband Brick were building a new house in Smithfield, and Ava said she had rather go see it and chat with the construction workers. And that's what she did.

At another time, Jack hosted a dinner party for Ava at one of the best steak houses in North Carolina. His purpose for the expensive evening was to treat his famous sister to a fine steak. But the only thing she ordered was an inch-thick slice of onion with French dressing.

Jack had became successful in business, and at forty-five he married for the first time. His wife, Rose, was much younger than he, and the marriage ended in separation after a few years. Jack was elected to the Smithfield Board of Commissioners in 1965 and became Mayor Pro-Tem two years later. Elected to the state legislature in 1970, he would serve several terms.

Ava would make only six films during the 1960s, the most notable Tennessee Williams' *The Night of the Iguana* with Richard Burton, the story of two very different women who were in love with a fallen man of the cloth. Some critics considered this her finest performance. She received a Golden Globe nomination as Best Actress of 1964 but didn't win.

Two years later Ava would make *The Bible* with George C. Scott. She became involved in a relationship with Scott, a heavy drinker, that ended after he became abusive.

It didn't bother Ava to be making fewer films. She often said that being a movie star was "a big damn bore." She kept going before the cameras, she said, for only one reason: "For the loot, Honey, only for the loot." Although not extremely rich, Ava had managed her earnings well, and tabloid reports that she was supported by Frank Sinatra, from whom she had taken no alimony, were false.

After *Night of the Iguana* came out, Ava came to New York and stayed at the Regency Hotel. While there, she invited Verlia Creech to come to the city and spend a couple of days with her.

Verlia and Ava's nephew Al Creech had been divorced for

several years by then, and Al had married again and had a daughter, Bonnie.

Verlia later would marry again, too, but she was still single when she went to New York to see Ava. She arrived to find Ava soaking in a bubble bath. In an adjoining bathroom another tubful of bubbles was waiting for Verlia.

"I'd had a bath just a few hours earlier," she remembered, "but I got undressed and into my bubble bath." Ava took Verlia to the famed jazz club Birdland. "It was a cold night, and we were going to walk the short distance from the hotel," Verlia recalled. "Ava insisted that I wear her leopard skin coat. It went almost all the way to the floor and must have weighed fifty pounds."

Not one to leave any detail of hospitality to chance, Ava had arranged for Verlia to have famous comedian Louie Nye as her escort that night. Ava's escort was her secretary, a handsome young man named Ed Schaefer.

Before they left the hotel, Ava handed Verlia a pair of ballet slippers and told her to slip them into her purse. She didn't explain why.

A fine band was playing that night, and Ava told Verlia to pay attention to one of the musicians. Ava thought he was excellent, and it bothered her that audience members always sought out the other band members for praise.

Ava told Verlia to take the ballet slippers to the ignored musician and ask him to autograph them.

And she did.

Verlia's visit ended on a less than happy note. Ava brought her two Welsh corgis with her to New York, one quite old, and during Verlia's visit, the older one turned up missing.

After a frantic search, the beloved pet was found behind a pair of heavy red drapes, alive but in poor condition. Ava summoned a veterinarian but the dog did not recover.

"Ava was very distraught," Verlia recalled.

When *The Bible* came out, Ava came again to New York, and while she was there a long-time fan, Andrew Anthos, arranged for her to meet Barney Duhan, who had seen her photo in the window of her brother-in-law's photography studio and unknowingly launched her career.

Duhan became a police officer after leaving Loews Theatres, studied law at night, and later opened a law office on Broadway. After meeting Ava, who was forty-three at the time, he said he was impressed not only by her enduring natural beauty, but by her warmth and down-to-earth personality.

After Ava had been in Spain for twelve years, the government hit her with a huge tax bill. She'd always paid her taxes faithfully and thought that her disgruntled neighbor Juan Peron may have had a hand in this turn of events.

As much as she loved Spain, she decided time had come for her to go, and in 1968 she moved to London. She found a luxury apartment in Ennismore Gardens that would become her home for the rest of her life.

She came to love London. The press didn't bother her, and only now and then did anybody recognize her as she walked her dog Morgan, a Welsh corgi named for Ava's business manager, Jess Morgan.

By this point, Ava had pretty much given up the nightlife, and although she became increasingly reclusive, she had no lack of companionship. Close friends, such as Charles Gray, lived nearby and she frequently went out to dinner with them. Reenie came for extended stays, and occasionally Ava had visitors from home.

Thomas J. "Tom" Lassiter, editor of *The Smithfield Herald*, and his wife "Lib" were two of those visitors in June of 1974.

Before they left, Bappie's ex-husband, William I. Godwin, gave them Ava's phone number and told them to give her a call.

William was then called Judge Godwin. He was a district court judge and his juvenile court had been lauded as the best in North Carolina. He later would be elected mayor of Selma and would die in 1976 at seventy-four from a stroke he suffered while visiting at the home of Ava's sister Inez.

Tom and Lib hadn't seen Ava since the 1949 dance in her honor, and not wishing to intrude on her privacy, they were reluctant to bother her.

117

"But Tom finally got up the nerve to call," Lib recalled. "Ava was not at home at the time, but her maid took the message that we were staying at the Hyde Park Hotel."

When the Lassiters returned to the hotel the desk clerk announced that they had a message from Ava Gardner, who requested that they return her call.

As it turned out, Ava had plans that evening, and the Lassiters were to have dinner with P.W.E. Taylor, a barrister and counsel to the Queen. The Lassiters knew Taylor's sister, Sybil Champion, who lived in Clayton in Johnston County.

Ava insisted that Tom and Lib come to her apartment for cocktails.

Ava was dressed for dinner when they arrived. "She had on an eggshell outfit and a matching turban," Lib recalled, "and she was absolutely beautiful."

They found her eager for news about her family and friends at home. She also had an avid interest in the Watergate scandal, and had been keeping up with it on TV. She had become a great admirer of North Carolina's Senator Sam Ervin, who was presiding over the hearings.

Ava had sent Senator Sam a photo of herself and had autographed it: "To a country lawyer from a country girl."

She proudly showed off an autographed photo she had received in return from Senator Sam.

Before they left, Tom asked if Ava would mind if he wrote something about their visit for his newspaper.

"Listen, I don't care what you write, as long as you tell the truth," Ava said.

Rock Ridge Reunion

In the spring of 1978, Ava attended the wedding of Princess Caroline, daughter of her old friend Grace Kelly, who had given up her acting career to marry Prince Ranier of Monaco.

Ava was one of few guests with links to Princess Grace's Hollywood past to be invited to the wedding.

After leaving Monaco, Ava came to North Carolina for a family visit and to reluctantly attend a May reunion of Rock Ridge High School alumni.

The reunion was being held in conjunction with Rock Ridge Day, which was marking the transition of the school to elementary grades only. Another graduate of Rock Ridge, Class of '55, North

Governor Jim Hunt, another graduate of Rock Ridge School, spoke at reunion at which Ava was honored in 1978.

Carolina Governor James B. Hunt Jr., was a guest of honor.

Ava's reluctance to attend the reunion was largely because of her ever-increasing fear of facing crowds. But there were other reasons as well.

She was now the same age her mother was when the two moved into the Rock Ridge Teacherage thirty-nine years earlier. She was afraid she would disappoint her former schoolmates, and therefore be disappointed herself. Still she agreed to come.

But when luggage containing the outfit Ava intended to wear to the reunion didn't arrive with her, and transportation she was promised by the governor's office didn't show up, she backed out.

When Ava told Emily Sheffield and her son Dewey that she wasn't coming, their disappointment was obvious. But after much pleading from Dewey, Ava's brother Jack and finally from Governor Hunt, she gave in and said she would go. The next day, she changed her mind again. She was not going, and that was that. She was supposed to read a formal proclamation for Rock Ridge Day, and she was afraid she would be so nervous that she would stumble over the words. Movie scenes could be shot over and over, but public speaking offered only one shot. She didn't have time enough to rehearse, she said, and she couldn't and wouldn't do it. She would not go.

Dewey Sheffield came to Smithfield and sat down with Ava.

Dewey Sheffield Jr. (foreground) was Ava's escort at reunion.
Deputy Ronnie Batchelor is at left.

Ava and Emily Sheffield, her mother's dear friend,
at a dinner party hosted by Jack.

Ava went into the crowd to bring Dewey Sheffield Sr. to the stage.

Ava greets her best high school friend, Alberta Cooney Luehrs, whom she hadn't seen in nearly 39 years.

Using a Flair pen, he divided some of the proclamation's tongue-tangling terminology into syllables so they would be easier to get through.

Ava agreed to go if Dewey would be her driver and escort. She wore tan slacks, a long-sleeved red-and-white striped blouse with a white collar and a tan necktie.

Seated on the outdoor dias with Governor Hunt and other honorees, Ava held a small lollipop which she discreetly placed in her mouth now and then to keep it moist while awaiting her turn to speak.

When she stepped to the podium, she opened her arms in acknowledgement of the enthusiastic reception, then began to talk of her days at Rock Ridge. She called Emily Sheffield to her side, put her arm around her, and told the gathering how much she had meant to her and her mother.

Her reading of the Rock Ridge Day proclamation was flawless, and afterward she was swamped by old friends and admirers. Standing at the edge of the throng was Ava's best friend from high school days, Alberta Cooney Luehrs. Someone urged her to push her way up to Ava, but she said no.

"I didn't know if Ava would even remember me, or if she would recognize me with my gray hair," Alberta said.

Then Ava turned her head and their eyes met for the first time in nearly forty years. A highway patrolman was standing near Ava, and she turned to him and said, "Please move the crowd back just a little, so I can get to Alberta."

As the two old friends embraced, it was almost as if they had never parted, Alberta remembered.

Ava asked Alberta to write to her and tell her all about her life, and she promised to do the same.

On her way out of the school grounds, Ava asked Dewey to stop the car. She had spotted Alberta's mother. She reached out the car window, took Bertha Hinnant's hand, and told her she remembered all the wonderful times she had in her home, as well as her delicious ham biscuits.

Back at Jack's house in Smithfield, Ava met with a reporter for *The Smithfield Herald*, (the author of this book), who found her barefoot, without makeup, not as tall as expected, but still beautiful, warm and witty.

Ava asked Jack to sit with her and hold her hand during the interview. She didn't want to say much about her career or personal life and spent most of the interview talking about those she considered to have accomplished great things in Hollywood. She refused to place herself in that category.

Then she moved to lighter things. Laughing, she told about a time when she and Bappie were on their way to an event honoring

Ava posed for *The Smithfield Herald* after Rock Ridge reunion.

director George Cukor and had a flat tire. Another car pulled in behind them and out stepped Katharine Hepburn. She opened her trunk, Ava remembered, whipped out some tools, changed the tire, and went on her way.

Ava also talked about how much she loved being back in Johnston County. She liked to lie under the pine trees in Jack's back yard and listen to the birds, she said.

"I feel at peace here."

When picture-taking time came, Ava told the reporter, "Let me give you a tip that a famous photographer once passed along to me. The best portraits are the ones in which the subject is not smiling."

But the readers of *The Smithfield Herald* saw a shot of Ava barefoot and smiling.

Alberta did write to Ava, and asked for a current photo. Ava responded soon thereafter.

Dear Alberta

Finally got a picture for you. Sorry it's got a big hat on. It's one I had made for that Roy Bean thing (Ava had a cameo role in *The Life and Times of Judge Roy Bean* with Paul Newman in 1972.). *I'm going to (have) some made of "me" soon & I'll send you one. I keep threatening to have some made but always find some excuse not to. It was so good to see you again after all these years. I'd forgotten what beautiful eyes you have. Maybe when I get home the next time we can get together for a few snorts. I'm to do a week's work in Montreal in Sept. so I'll try to get home for a few days. London has been miserable this summer. Worst we've had in ten years & I'm sick to death of lousey rain. Today is the first sunny day in about three weeks. Cara my little pooch & I just got back from Hyde Park & it's so beautiful when it's a nice day. I'm enclosing a snap that was taken the night I went to the ball for Grace Kelly's daughter. I really did look pretty & it's the only photo made. If I'd looked like hell there would have been a million photographers around.*

Hope to see you soon
Love to your mama & much love to you
Ava

Thus began a correspondence that would continue for as long as Ava lived.

The Trying Eighties

The 1980s would be the most difficult decade in Ava's life.

Her brother was elected to another term in the legislature in the fall of 1980, and was sworn in on January 14, 1981. Three hours later, he was dead of a stroke at sixty-nine.

Ava didn't come to the funeral, for fear that her presence would turn the service into a circus.

She told Emily Sheffield that she would be in church during the time that Jack's funeral was being held in Smithfield's First Presbyterian Church. He was buried in the Gardner family plot in Sunset Memorial Park.

Only six weeks later, Ava's sister Inez died of diabetic complications. She was seventy-four. She was buried in Sunset Memorial Park beside her husband Johnnie, who had died in September, 1973, after suffering from a disorder that caused paralysis and loss of speech.

Ava had made only eight movies in the 1970s, with no roles of any significance, and she was soon to make her final films for the big screen.

In 1981, she played Mable Dodge Luhan, patron of author D.H. Lawrence in *Priest of Love* with Ian McKellan, Janet Suzman, and Sir John Gielgud. She received critical acclaim for her performance, and there was speculation that she might have received another Academy Award nomination if the film had been more widely distributed. Few moviegoers had a chance to see it, and even fewer would have a chance to see her next, and final, for theatrical distribution.

Ava filmed *Regina* in Italy in 1983 with Anthony Quinn, and afterward even Ava didn't want to see it.

Although she didn't count TV as filmmaking, Ava returned to California in 1985 for seven guest appearances on the primetime CBS soap opera *Knots Landing*.

She played Ruth Sumner, mother of the ruthless lawyer, Greg Sumner, played by William Devane. And she was quickly taken to heart by Joan Van Ark and other stars of the show, who wanted her to stay on as a regular, but Ava declined.

"Nobody can imagine how hard those television series actors have to work," she told a friend. "I'm too old for that sort of thing."

She was sixty-two, and the supermarket tabloids were publishing unflattering photos of her and calling her an "aging actress."

Still, Ava starred that year in two made-for-television movies, *Harem* with Omar Sharif and *The Long, Hot Summer* with Jason Robards. Cybill Shepherd and Don Johnson also appeared in *The Long, Hot Summer*, and Don presented Ava a red rose each day during the filming.

In 1986, despite her concern about appearing in a regular TV series, Ava got talked into playing a supporting role in a CBS pilot, *Maggie*, starring Stefanie Powers as a detective. She had lost weight for the role and looked younger and more beautiful than she had for years. The series didn't get picked up, however. That pilot would be Ava's last appearance on film.

She returned to London, and shortly thereafter suffered a stroke, which left her left arm all but useless and made walking difficult.

She was brought to Los Angeles for treatment and stayed at Bappie's house in Nichols Canyon. Frank Sinatra sent a limousine each day to take her to the hospital for therapy.

•   •   •

Ava's last appearance on film was with Stefanie Powers, right, in 1986 TV pilot, *Maggie*, that was not picked up by the networks.

On January 29, 1987, Ava's sister Elsie Mae died at eighty-two. She was buried in Sunset Memorial Park beside her husband David and son Bobby, who had died at thirty-seven in 1969 of injuries from a car wreck.

Ava and Alberta kept up their correspondence. Alberta had sent Ava a photo of her two sons and her daughter and their spouses and children.

"I envy you," Ava wrote back.

Alberta had lost her first husband to cancer after forty years of marriage and had married again. She and her new husband, Ed Fagan, lived in Maryland, but later would move to North Carolina.

In 1988 after hearing that Ava was ill with severe respiratory problems, Alberta wrote to encourage her. Ava responded under trying circumstances.

Dear Alberta
Thank you so much honey for your letters of consern. I'm afraid there is not very good news healthwise. I'm on my way to California by air ambulance. Too sick to travel otherwise. Sometimes I think it would be better to be born sick & miserable than to know a healthy good life & have it snatched away in two weeks.

Anyway enough of that. I wish you a very Happy & good New Year.
   With much Love
   Ava

Ava's jagged handwriting indicated the effort she had put forth to write.

"It meant so much to know that she wanted to write the letters herself, rather than have her secretary do it for her," Alberta said.

In January, 1990, after Alberta wrote to tell Ava of the birth of another grandchild, she received another brief letter from Ava in handwriting even more strained.

Dear Alberta
   I hope your granddaughter's name is Emily. You didn't say in the letter. It's always good to hear from you. I hope you (are) well and happy. I'm still a mess after yet another bout of double pneumonia & no left hand! It's a bitch.
I send you lots of love.

                              Ava

The next news Alberta would receive of Ava would come only days later, and it would be news she didn't want to hear.

A note to her friend Alberta written only days before Ava's death.

Coming Home to Stay

Ava's great niece, Ava Carol Creech Thompson, a high school principal with three children, was taking a shower at her home in JohnstonCounty shortly before six a.m. on January 25, 1990, when her son Neal called to her that she had a phone call from London.

"I knew Ava was planning a trip home," Ava Carol said, "and I thought she was calling to tell us she had finalized her plans."

But when she picked up the phone, she heard the hysterical voice of Ava's housekeeper, Carmen Vargas. At first she had difficulty understanding Carmen because of her broken English, but Ava Carol finally realized what Carmen was trying to tell her: Ava was dead.

A man suddenly came on the line, identified himself as a physician, and confirmed the news. Ava was being treated for double pneumonia. Carmen had brought breakfast to her bed, and when she returned to pick up the tray, Ava had stopped breathing. She was sixty-seven.

None of Ava's family knew that she was so sick. Like her mother before her, she had kept her dire symptoms to herself.

The death of Ava Gardner was front-page news around the globe. It was the cover story in *People* magazine, with the headline "The Last Goddess."

Paris Match magazine, Europe's equivalent of *Life*, assigned a photographer to cover the funeral and later published forty-two pages of pictures tracing Ava's life and career.

A distraught Carmen accompanied Ava's body home to North Carolina. It was in a light-colored coffin shaped like a body when it arrived at Underwood Funeral Home in Smithfield. The coffin had a window so part of Ava's face could be seen. Fastened on the lid was a small metallic label on which her name was misspelled "Gardener."

The Gardner family had the body transferred to a beautiful casket of polished cherry, and only family members were allowed to view it. Bappie was not there. She'd had a foot amputated only days earlier due to diabetes and was in a nursing home in California. Ava's sister Myra was devastated. Her husband Bronnie Pearce had died ten days before Ava.

Friends and fans were allowed to pay their respects on the night before the funeral. Some 3,000 people passed by Ava's closed coffin. Yellow roses, Ava's favorites, had been the first flowers to arrive, sent by her old friend Lena Horne.

A massive arrangement came with a card that read, "With my love, Francis." (Ava liked to tease Frank Sinatra with his formal name.) Frank personally phoned in the order to a flower shop operated by Barbara Twiggs near Smithfield.

Ava's graveside service was held in Sunset Memorial Park on January 29, 1990, and was conducted by the Rev. Francis Bradshaw, pastor of Smithfield's Centenary United Methodist Church.

A crowd of about 500 attended, and the air was filled with the sound of clicking cameras.

Seated with family members under a graveside tent, Carmen Vargas wept openly.

When a limousine with tinted windows pulled into the cemetery and parked a short distance behind the throng, a buzz spread through the crowd. Was Frank Sinatra in that car?

One man who passed close by it said he felt certain he had seen beefy bodyguards behind the darkened glass. But the occupants of the limousine turned out to be a hairdresser and several friends from Fayetteville who wanted to attend the funeral of a Hollywood legend in a style they deemed fitting.

No celebrities came to Ava's funeral, no doubt for the same reason that she did not attend the funeral of her brother Jack. They didn't want to mar the dignity of the proceedings by having the focus turn to them.

A light rain started to fall just before the service began, and black umbrellas opened over those standing beyond the shelter of the tent.

A movie buff whispered to a friend, "It's just like the opening scene in *The Barefoot Contessa*."

At the close of the brief service, the sun broke through. As she had requested, Ava's body was laid to rest beside her brother, close by her mother and father in the family plot.

Her footstone was engraved only with her name and dates of birth and death, according to her instructions.

The flowers that were massed atop Ava's grave when the family returned after the interment were soon stripped away by souvenir-seekers, leaving the gravesite as bare as the winter fields at Grabtown as they awaited the coming of spring.

But Ava's grave would rarely be void of flowers in years to come. Family and friends brought them regularly, as did fans who came from throughout the world. One woman who arrived empty-handed went to her car and brought back the only thing she had to offer: a small pumpkin. Surely the country girl that Ava remained in her heart would have appreciated that tribute.

The simple footstone Ava requested for her grave in Sunset Memorial Park in Smithfield.

Back to Her Sister's Side

After being a divorcee since the early 1940s, Bappie had married again in the late 1950s. Her third husband, Art Cole, was properties manager for Desilu Studios. They were married for about ten years before his death.

Bappie lived until November 6, 1993, only eight days from her ninetieth birthday. She died in a California nursing home. She was brought home to Johnston County and buried beside Ava, whose life she had helped to mold, and to whose side she'd always come in times of need.

With Bappie's death, Myra was the last surviving offspring of Jonas and Mollie Gardner, and she sought solace in memories. She began thinking of her brother Raymond, killed by a dynamite cap four years before she was born.

She had never been to Raymond's grave, and now she felt a strong urge to go. Myra and her niece Mary Edna Grantham got directions to the isolated family cemetery in Pitt County from distant kin and found it, overgrown with weeds and briars, after traipsing through a cornfield.

They didn't know what kind of marker, if any, had been placed on the grave, but Mary Edna said she knew it the moment she saw it from a distance.

A pink wild rose vine had entwined the winged cherub that Jonas and Mollie placed on the grave.

The two women were deeply moved by their discovery in that lonely spot, and later Myra had the tombstone moved to the Gardner family plot in Smithfield so her family could be united, at least symbolically.

• • •

Frank Sinatra survived Ava by more than eight years, dying on May 14, 1998. At his death, he was hailed around the world as "Entertainer of the Century."

In the mid-1970s, Frank had called Ava and asked if they couldn't try again to make it as husband and wife. Even though she loved him, Ava told him, she knew it could never work. Not long afterward, Frank married Barbara Marx.

Three months after Frank's death, a near-life-size bronze statue of Ava was erected in the picturesque village of Tossa de Mar in Spain, where she filmed *Pandora and the Flying Dutchman* in 1950. Created by acclaimed Spanish sculptress Cio' Abelli, the sculpture stands on a high balcony. Ava is portrayed as Pandora, gazing toward the sea, her long hair and filmy garment forever caressed by the breeze. She is, appropriately, barefoot.

As the year 2000 approached, a survey of entertainment writers and editors placed Ava among the top twenty-five female movie stars of all time, and *People* magazine featured Ava and Frank as one of the century's greatest love stories.

A statue of Ava as "Pandora" was erected in the village of Tossa de Mar in Spain in 1998.

The Ava Gardner Museum

Tommy Banks, the boy Ava playfully kissed on the cheek on the Atlantic Christian College campus, eventually become Dr. Thomas M. Banks, a clinical psychologist in Pompano Beach, Florida.

The clipping from *The Wilson Daily Times* that he placed in a shoe box in 1941 had ballooned into an Ava Gardner memorabilia collection that was taking up every spare inch of the condominium he shared with his wife, Lorraine, a school librarian.

From its simple beginning, Tom's hobby had continued without pause. During his years as a student at the College of William and Mary, Ava was named his Fraternity Sweetheart, and he began an on-going correspondence with her. When he served as an intelligence officer in the Navy, his sister, Katherine Banks Brittingham, kept clipping items about Ava and pasting them in scrapbooks for him.

So enchanted by Ava was Tom that in 1949, he went to Hollywood and worked as a publicist for *My Forbidden Past*, in which Ava co-starred with Robert Mitchum.

By the late 1970s, his memorabilia collection had grown so huge that friends in Florida often wondered why his wife put up with it. Lorraine responded that she was well aware of her husband's hobby when she married him, so she just gave in and began helping with it. She'd come to care as much about Ava as he did.

In 1979, Tom took part of his collection to Smithfield and exhibited it for three days. He brought back more the following year. While there he added appreciably to his collection by buying the old Brogden School Teacherage, which had served as a community center for a while, but had been abandoned for years.

In 1981, Tom moved his entire collection to the building and opened it that summer as the Ava Gardner Museum.

In coming years, Tom and Lorraine returned to Brogden and kept the museum open through the summer. As word spread about it, fans from around the world came to see his amazing collection. Some arrived upset.

Tom didn't want the museum to intrude on its rural environs and insisted that no directional signs be erected. The sign in front of the building said only, "The Teacherage." Some people wandered for hours through the countryside looking for it.

Ava's four sisters came together to see the museum, and were astounded by the collection's magnitude.

"I had no idea Ava made this many movies!" Myra said.

"Ava has got to come to see this," Tom told her sisters.

As new items were added to the exhibit, Tom sent photos of them to Ava. At the end of each summer season, he sent her a copy of the guest register, on which visitors had written notes for her.

Ava did visit the museum when she came home to see family in the spring of 1985.

She and three of her sisters, Bappie, Elsie Mae, and Myra, rode out to see the family home in Grabtown, then went on to Brogden. The old Brogden School, which had closed in 1961, was just a crumbling shell then. It had been gutted by fire at the beginning of the year. The Teacherage, along with Tom's amazing collection might have been lost if the Brogden Volunteer Fire Department hadn't been just across the road.

The museum door was padlocked when Ava and her sisters arrived. "We can call a museum volunteer and have her bring a key," Myra suggested.

But Ava nixed that idea. She didn't want to bother anyone. "I know what's in there," she said. "I lived it."

Tom was deeply disappointed when he learned that Ava had gone to the museum but didn't go inside. He sent word to Ava that if she'd let him know the next time she came, he'd fly up and meet her.

Tom would not get that opportunity. He suffered a stroke at the museum in August, 1989, and died in Duke University Hospital nine days later. His death came as a shock. He was sixty-two but looked much younger and appeared to be in perfect health. Ava sent a telegram to Lorraine expressing her condolences.

Lorraine buried some of her husband's ashes in the Banks family plot in Wilson. She scattered the rest on the grounds of The Teacherage.

Before Tom's death, he and Lorraine had purchased tickets for a tour of England. Friends urged Lorraine to go ahead with the plans. Her friend Jean Childers of Pompano Beach offered to go with her.

Years earlier, Tom and Lorraine had gone to the Netherlands to see a painter named Adlebert Pfeiffer. As a teenager during World War II, Pfeiffer had been a prisoner in a Nazi concentration camp. He later attended art school in The Hague, and while there he contracted a rare disease that caused his fingers to draw into fists and freeze in that position.

He earned a living by holding a paint brush in his fist and producing portraits of local residents in the small town of Panningen. In 1948, after Ava appeared in *One Touch of Venus*, Pfeiffer painted a portrait of her, using a magazine photo as a guide. Although he never had any contact with Ava, he painted a portrait of her every year for the next fifty years, some of them life-size, all of them different. Tom and Lorraine purchased twenty-six of them and brought them back for their collection. Now Lorraine decided to take one to Ava as a gift when she and her friend went to England.

Lorraine sent photos to Ava so she could pick the one she wanted. But she sent back word that she didn't want one.

She wanted three!

Their visit, Lorraine reported, was wonderful.

"It was almost like three old school chums getting together," she said.

They were sipping wine when Ava started talking about Frank Sinatra, Lorraine remembered.

"Damn," Ava said, suddenly getting up. "I need a real drink."

And she poured a stiff one.

Lorraine had meant to bring some photos for Ava to sign, but had left them at her hotel. She asked if she could bring them the next day, and Ava said to bring them on.

But when Lorraine and her friend arrived the next day, Carmen told them that Ava was too sick for company.

They did not see her again.

Only a few months later, Ava was dead. Lorraine donated the Ava collection to the Town of Smithfield a year after Tom's death. It went on display in a rented building on South Third Street in the spring of 1991. The old Brogden Teacherage was sold and remodeled as a residence.

The first docent in the museum's new location was Marion Grimes Crayton, who had been Ava's playmate at Brogden, always dirtying the clothes her mother warned her not to soil. Marion was now sixty-eight, a widow and grandmother. Museum visitors enjoyed hearing her stories about Ava.

One day, a tall man with a scruffy gray beard and a cap pulled low on his head entered the museum. Two women came in at the same time and went to an exhibit where another docent, Deidre Kraft, was busy with other visitors.

Marion took the lone man on a tour.

"In 1949, Ava wore this gown in *The Great Sinner* with Gregory Peck," she said when they came to a black velvet gown.

"Oh yes, I remember that gown," the man said.

Marion said she almost fainted when she heard that distinctive voice.

She was talking to Gregory Peck.

He had been filming a television movie in Raleigh, and the beard was for his role as an aging artist. The women who entered the museum with him were his wife, Veronique, and their driver.

Peck autographed several photos and posters in the collection and agreed to serve as Honorary National Chairman of the Museum committee.

Columnist Liz Smith, St. Clair Pugh, Lena Horne, and actress Elaine Stritch, all of whom hosted a benefit for the museum in New York in 1992, also served on the honorary committee, along with actor Roddy McDowall, another of Ava's devoted friends.

One indication of Gregory Peck's affection for Ava was something he did after her death. He brought her maid Carmen Vargas and her dog Morgan to Los Angeles to live in his guest house.

When Ava's beloved Morgan died, he buried him in his back yard.

In September, 1993, renowned jazz pianist and composer Loonis McGlohan of Charlotte brought his trio to Smithfield for a benefit concert for the museum.

Forty-three years earlier, Loonis had watched Ava leave the stage as a loser in a beauty contest in Tarboro. Now he debuted a lilting piano solo he had composed especially for the occasion.

It was titled simply "Ava."

In November, 2000, a new, upscale version of the Ava Gardner Museum opened in permanent quarters on Smithfield's Market Street.

The house in Grabtown in which Ava was born remains standing. Renovated, it is now the home of Bobby Ray Allen, who was born in the house in 1934, the year Ava and her parents moved to Newport News. The boarding house in Newport News was demolished many years ago. The Rock Ridge Teacherage, now in disrepair, is used for storage.

An upscale version of
Dr. Tom Banks' Ava
Gardner Museum opened
in Smithfield in
November, 2000.

Final Thoughts

Ava performed sixty-two roles in a film career that spanned forty-four years.

She endured in a profession in which only the strong survive. And she survived, not because she overcame her rural North Carolina background—but because she drew her strength from it.

Although Ava endured, she stubbornly insisted that she was "never an actress." And she said that movie stardom had given her everything she never wanted.

She would have been content with life as an average North Carolina housewife, she said, would have been happy with the love of a good husband who was a farmer or auto mechanic. She would have been happy with a houseful of children and chubby-cheeked grandchildren, and with cooking Sunday dinners of fried chicken, mashed potatoes, collards, cornbread, and banana pudding.

Some believed her when she said things like that, others thought she was only joking. And all knew it was pointless to ponder the "what ifs" of her life.

She followed her destiny.

Her family, friends, and fans can hope that the Grabtown Girl finally realized how much she had accomplished during her remarkable life. Ava Carol Thompson said she felt that as Ava grew older and had time to reflect, she did come to understand how much she had achieved, and was proud of her career. She was also proud that she had been able to remain financially independent through it all.

Those who knew, loved, and admired her most can hope that in her quiet reveries, she could still remember the sound of applause as the curtains swished to a close on her first-grade performance in the operetta at Brogden School.

They can hope that, in the still of a wintry London night, the sound of that applause rose ever higher and louder and traveled around the world, as Ava Lavenia Gardner, like Little Rose, ended her mortal journey through Fairyland—and came home to stay.

Ava Gardner Filmography

Movies

1942. *We Were Dancing; Joe Smith, American; Sunday Punch; This Time for Keeps; Kid Glove Killer; Mighty Lak a Goat*

1943. *Pilot No. 5, Hitler's Madman, Ghosts on the Loose, Young Ideas, The Lost Angel, Swing Fever*

1944. *Three Men in White, Maisie Goes to Reno*

1945. *She Went to the Races*

1946. *Whistle Stop, The Killers*

1947. *The Hucksters, Singapore*

1948. *One Touch of Venus*

1949. *The Bribe, The Great Sinner, East Side, West Side*

1951. *My Forbidden Past, Pandora and the Flying Dutchman, Show Boat*

1952. *Lone Star, The Snows of Kilimanjaro*

1953. *Ride, Vaquero!; Mogambo; The Band Wagon*

1954. *Knights of the Round Table, The Barefoot Contessa*

1956. *Bhowani Junction*

1957. *The Little Hut, The Sun Also Rises*

1959. *The Naked Maja, On the Beach*

1960. *The Angel Wore Red*

1963. *55 Days at Peking*

1964. *Seven Days in May, The Night of the Iguana*

1966. *The Bible*

1969. *Mayerling*

1970. *Tam Lin*

1972. *The Life and Times of Judge Roy Bean*

1974. *Earthquake, Permission to Kill*

1976. *The Blue Bird*

1977. *The Cassandra Crossing, The Sentinel*

1979. *City on Fire*

1980. *The Kidnapping of the President*

1981. *Priest of Love*

1983. *Regina*

Television

1985. *Knots Landing; A.D.; The Long, Hot Summer; Harem*

1986. *Maggie (pilot for series which was not picked up by networks.)*